D1418514

In the Hands of Angels

In the Hands
of Angels

PATRICIA M. CRAMER

CARMEL • NEW YORK 10512

This Guideposts edition is published by special arrangement with Mackinaw Bridge Publishing.

Jacket and interior designed by José R. Fonfrias

Library of Congress Catalog Card Number: 95-75305

ISBN: 1-886881-00-6

Contents

Contents

~ *Acknowledgments* ~

MY HEARTFELT APPRECIATION GOES FIRST TO *all of the people written about in this book* who opened up to me about the significant events of their lives especially because some had told very few others what had happened to them. My terrific *husband Dale* then deserves my thanks for realizing I needed a laptop computer, and for always sitting patiently beside me as I typed in planes, cars, restaurants, the office, and the kitchen. That computer literally became an extension of my arm to be opened on a moment's notice using even a few minutes of available time. *Mary Louise Luikens*, my mother, and *Theresa Stephens*, my sister, began to share my passion for angel activity as we talked endlessly about the people I had met and their incredible stories. *Sandra Rodkey* always listened to my progress and provided the most breathtaking and inspiring ocean view at a time when I needed quiet to create a large part of the text. *Theresa Weber* provided wonderful friendship and invaluable guidance at a very critical point in my writing, and *Heidi Hougham-Ream* continually encouraged me especially when she told me that reading these stories gave her comfort and consolation as her father lay dying. *Martina Stern*, my proofreader, checked the text carefully. *Reverends Fran and Bill Davis* excited me with their dedication to their angel ministry and Fran was especially helpful by sharing her angel library with me. *Marti Jacobs* lent her years of printing expertise to the prodigious task of producing a high-quality finished product.

The following people all provided some kind of support, encouragement or information resource, and I want them to know I appreciate them: *Dr. Jan Adams and Dr. Daryl Adams, Barbara Bourg Carpenter, Jane Carlton, Dr. Ed Colozzi and Linda Colozzi, Larry and Janet Cramer, Dr. Janet Elsea, Nancy Fox, Charlotte Knesek, Rosina McClellan, Jane McNair, Orpheus Phyllos, Marcia Reynolds, Joe and Judy Sabah, David Scott Taylor, Elaine Ulrich, and Betty Webb.*

∼ *Foreword* ∼

"BE NOT FORGETFUL TO ENTERTAIN STRANGERS, for thereby some have entertained angels unawares." Hebrews 13:2.

From this biblical quote we have had many "earth angels" appear in our lives. Whether you call these encounters "serendipitous" or "coincidence," we have found much more. An old quote states, "Coincidence is God's way of remaining anonymous." God may remain anonymous but sends his angels to make many appearances.

Our first encounter with Pat Cramer was when Bill and I sent out flyers for an angel seminar. A friend who had received the flyer called and said, "I know someone who should come to your presentation." She gave us Pat's name and we faxed her our flyer. Pat came, took copious notes, and then we talked. We realized we were entertaining a real, live, working angel. And our friendship continues to grow. Oddly enough, the friend who gave us Pat's name didn't make it to the seminar.

This intriguing book, *In the Hands of Angels,* is truly a volume of lessons categorized so that each chapter is a mini-volume in itself. There are lessons in trust, gratitude, serenity, hope, belief and surrender, to name a few. Pat has provided a checklist at the end of each chapter for you to write your thoughts. As you read the encounters of others, you may relate to an experience you had that you did not realize was "heaven-sent." Pat has done years of research, met many people, and is generous in sharing this knowledge with others.

Our paths in many ways have been similar. While Pat was interviewing people for this book, Bill and I were sharing the little gold angel pins you see many people wearing. We started our Regarding Angels Ministry when a friend pinned an angel on our shoulders and said, "Pass this on when you find someone who needs it." In five years, with the help of friends and angel ambassadors, we have distributed almost 50,000 of these tiny symbols of hope, peace, and love throughout the world. Through angel presentations and correspondence many lives have been touched. Although I have never seen an angel (but Bill has), we feel their presence guiding and guarding us along this fascinating path we now travel.

As it says in Psalm 91:11-12 "For he shall give his angels charge over thee, to keep thee in all thy ways. They shall bear thee up in their hands, lest thou dash thy foot against a stone." And those who read this book will gain a better understanding of the role the angels play in their lives and find they are truly "In the Hands of Angels."

Revs. Fran and Bill Davis
Regarding Angels Ministry
P. O. Box 1241
Gilbert, AZ 85299-1241
(602) 926-8641

~ *Preface* ~

THE PEOPLE YOU WILL MEET in this book are White, Native American, Hispanic, African American, and Asian. They are old and young, men and women, of every age group, and from almost every occupation practiced in this country. They share one universal characteristic: each has experienced something extraordinary, a life has been touched in a way in which it is forever altered.

While some of the stories you will read are almost miraculous, others are very simple—a tiny voice inside the head, a series of circumstances that appear to be somewhat coincidental, except that the recipient is convinced that a greater purpose underlies the occurrence. People speak of a faith that is strengthened, hope that is restored, and a peace and tranquility that pervades the everyday events of their lives after they have been touched by the angels. These are lessons we all must learn about living a more enlightened life—one where greater awareness leads to a sense of peace and joy empowered by love. This empowerment creates a sense of responsibility for everyone and everything around us, gives us hope that we can create a better world, and helps us to trust when we are afraid because we know we are not alone.

You may be thinking, "Well, I've certainly never met an angel." But after reading these stories of very ordinary people, you may recognize something that indeed has occurred to you. A thought, an urge, an insight may have taken you in a direction that has affected the circumstances of your life. A warning may have kept you out of danger, or a burst of strength and power may have been the needed help to resolve a situation. At the very least, you will be more fully aware of any future opportunity to heed a cautionary warning, encounter a helper, or use a guide.

You will find a place in each section to record in the form of a journal, your memories of incidents you haven't thought of in a long time that taught you the lessons learned by the people in this book. Perhaps situations that you took for granted or that seemed strange but not relevant at the time will help you recognize the steps you have already taken toward greater personal and spiritual empowerment. The recognition of these lessons may be the stimulus to even greater awareness of the availability of spiritual resources for your life.

To all of you who shared your special meetings, guiding messages, and moments of protection with me, especially those who said, "I've never told anyone about this before because they would think I was crazy" —**thank you** for your candor, for your trust, and for your willingness to inspire others. The readers who share for one brief moment a small piece of your life will now be more sensitive perhaps to be better able to see the many blessings that result from listening to and asking for assistance from heavenly companions.

HOW TO USE THIS BOOK

This volume gives you examples of real-life, practical experiences that people have had, and then a place to apply the ideas to your own life. Each chapter has a general theme reflected in the stories, followed by thoughts of how the lessons of that theme affect us, and then specific questions about how that lesson may have already occurred in your own life. Use a journal to make notes and record thoughts that come to you spontaneously. Your guardian angels and guides are teaching you and inspiring you through those insights, and you can use that knowledge for personal and spiritual growth.

~ *Introduction* ~

ANGELS SEEM TO BE EVERYWHERE TODAY. There are television specials, and serial programs, books, tapes, seminars, posters, greeting cards, artwork, jewelry, bumper stickers, entire stores devoted to angel merchandise, articles in newspapers and magazines, and televised segments on programs that are usually devoted to news and documentary or social commentary issues. The cover of Time magazine even carried a "picture" of an angel. That is a lot of attention for something you can't see. Or can you?

Frank saw a red-bearded stranger who appeared and then disappeared in front of his eyes, and warned him of an impending plane crash. Toni L. saw a filthy transient who spoke with a heavenly voice and inspired her to change her life. Leslie F. saw a mysterious diver who appeared from underwater, saved her from drowning, and disappeared...all without any tanks or other visible air supply. Halli M. had a parent who received accurate information about the results of an upcoming surgery scheduled for the next day from a person dressed in white—a hospital employee her mother thought—but someone who could never again be found or even identified as belonging to the staff. Halli also personally encountered a very tall policewoman who appeared suddenly on a deserted and ice-covered hill very late at night to push her car to safety. A Missouri heart attack patient was awakened from a near-fatal coma by a man with an armspread of fifteen feet. A mysterious Marine aided at the scene of an accident and appeared again later to guide a driver asleep at the wheel of a car. An "encyclopedia salesman" with a gentle, caring demeanor comforted a destitute young mother who was nearing despair over her circumstances, helped her forgive the people who had harmed her, and then walked down her driveway disappearing into thin air.

Hundreds of other normal, everyday people have not necessarily seen someone or something physical, but have been protected in a moment of extreme peril, guided when confused or uncertain, or warned of an imminent danger in time to do something about it by a message that came in the form of a thought, a feeling, or a touch. Angels seem to carry out their missions in very subtle ways, for which we need to develop a quite different set of eyes, ears, and perceptions.

The place to find an angel or guide is not always in the extraordinary, dangerous situation, but also in the ordinary events of our lives where the mundane is transformed into the miraculous. It requires opening our eyes and our hearts in a new way to learn a lesson that will empower our lives. You'll be inspired by the examples of the men, women, and children in this book who are of all ages and occupations and yet who each experienced some kind of guiding, leading, or helping hand.

Most of them were in awe of the help received, a few did not understand the significance of what had happened, some had no explanation whatsoever and were more puzzled, and a few felt it may just have been a series of coincidences or just plain "dumb luck." Each person who opened his or her awareness to the wondrous nature of the gift received experienced a deeper perspective of some aspect of his or her life. This "life lesson" then affected other encounters as each person grew spiritually.

Every reader of this book can reflect upon the special encounters or lessons that he or she has received, or can seek in a more focused way a future experience. By writing down the thoughts you have as you read these examples, tremendous insights will flow to you and your life will also move toward transformation. The only requirement is openness to a new experience and the dedication to learn from it.

While there are those who refuse to accept any "supernatural" influences in their lives, there are many more who readily accept and even ask for and welcome angelic encounters in their lives. Much can be learned from connecting with a spiritual Being who operates with a consciousness very different from that of a human. Regardless of whether a person is grateful, reluctant, searching, or rejecting, angel hands will still reach out, take ours, and leave us in some way forever changed because of the encounter. We are truly "transformed."

* * *

Why do angels visit? In the Bible, where slightly more than three hundred specific passages mention angels, the purpose of interaction with human beings was to bring information as a messenger, to guide or lead, to prevent harm, or to warn of a future event. While angels exist primarily to glorify God, they also seem to be hard workers constantly on the job helping to bring humans closer to God.

People say that the result of encountering an angel is often to strengthen or deepen faith, create hope, or receive an encouragement of the spirit when times are tough and prospects are dim. In the chaotic world today, people genuinely need a source of hope to avoid giving way to the despair evident all around us. Robert Kennedy is given credit for adapting something said originally by George Bernard Shaw into the famous quote about his brother, John— "Some people look at things as they are and ask why. My brother looked at things as they should be and asked why not?" It requires a fundamental shift in thinking for people to stop looking at things as they are—war, drugs, homelessness, rampant diseases such as AIDS, disintegrated families, increasing crime, and terrible natural disasters—asking "Why?"; and start looking at small miracles in daily life with a sense of optimism and expectation, an uplifting of the human spirit, asking in wonderment— "Why not?"

When we learn again to adopt a childlike sense of awe at how we are taught, rescued, protected, and warned by Helpers who first and foremost are considering our best interests, we will experience many more examples of their interaction. We will also discover lessons that will move us toward a path of enlightenment in our own lives, creating unparalleled emotional and spiritual growth.

Angels at My Side

A Lesson in Gratitude

 BEGAN THINKING AGAIN about the importance of the actions of angels in ordinary human lives after an encounter on an airplane several years ago. Although I have always believed in the existence of angelic beings and even have strong affection for ones that are personal friends and helpers, it was mostly a private conviction and I had not thought of speaking out publicly about them to a wide audience. At Los Angeles International Airport, I received a wake-up call that led ultimately to talking to all of the people who appear in this book.

It also led me to reflect on how the unusual encounters we have can teach us many important lessons about personal and spiritual growth—life lessons that raise our consciousness to a realm beyond the one we see with physical eyes. I realized how grateful we need to be for receiving the gift of help and guidance from angelic beings, a gift that sadly we often ignore or take for granted. My commitment now is to look at each day with a fresh sense of optimism and to learn the insights needed to constantly look beyond the obvious. I am trying to learn to always be thankful for the many small urgings and leadings from guardian spirits, my angels, who help me in so many ways.

The beginning of the journey to create this book was in an airplane arriving at a gate at Los Angeles International Airport (LAX). The flight had been delayed earlier, so many people on that plane were worried about missing connections, and the stress level was fairly high... The pilot made an announcement that any passengers who were not trying to make a tight connection should please remain seated so that others could get out quickly. For once, I was not one of the stressed-out, hurrying passengers because I was staying in Los Angeles that night to present a seminar the next day. I knew exactly what emotions the others were feeling, however, so in my mind I said, "I'll stay in my seat and let them get past. I'm certainly not in any hurry." Since I was sitting in an aisle seat, that would be my small contribution to not stand up and block the passageway. It is important to understand that my *conscious intention* was to stay seated.

The pilot turned off the "Fasten seat belt" sign and sounded the tone that allows everyone to stand up and start moving. I stayed seated...for about five seconds, until I found myself being literally pushed up out of my seat by the equivalent of a giant hand. As it was happening, I was thinking, "What on earth am I doing? I was going to stay put." I was genuinely puzzled about my behavior, not stepping into the aisle but standing straight up in front of my seat.

The very next second, a heavy briefcase weighing at least twenty pounds that had shifted during the flight fell out of the overhead bin, brushing my back as it passed, and landed with a soft "thunk" in the seat I had just vacated. As I turned and picked it up to hand it to the passenger behind me who had opened the bin, I looked at the metal-studded corners, felt the very hefty weight of the case, and realized with horror that if I had stayed in my seat as intended, I would have had my head bashed in.

It was sobering to realize that the falling object would probably have killed me since it would have caught me squarely on the top of my head; it was heavy enough anyway, and would have added weight with the momentum of its fall. I sat back down weakly for a moment, grateful that I was unharmed, uttered a brief prayer of thanks, and finally left the plane. It was shortly after that when I began to think more deeply about why things happen the way they do.

After the plane incident, I felt that I was being specifically protected from danger and began to think about the many ways that I had been helped in my life, that had not always seemed so obvious at the time they occurred. When I was ten years old, I was swimming at a community pool in a city park. My eight-year old brother had joined me for the open swim time in the afternoon after the "girls' lesson" which I had attended, and he said that he wanted to jump off the diving board in the deep end but he was afraid. Now the "deep end" was twelve feet since this was an Olympic-sized pool with a three-meter "high diving" platform and a one-meter diving board. I said to him, "Well go ahead and do it, I'll catch you."

I saw Tom climbing the high platform (as I recall now, I hadn't realized he had meant the higher board; I thought he was going to use the lower diving board) and swam over somewhat apprehensively to where I was positioned below and to the front of the platform. He jumped and landed directly on top of me and grabbed onto me in his fear.

Unfortunately, he had pinned my arms to my sides as he wrapped his around me so I didn't have much to work with to help us float and the two of us sank like a rock from the force of his jump. I know we were near the bottom because I was kicking my feet furiously to help us rise, and I was scraping my toes on the concrete bottom—I later found raw, bleeding spots.

The harder I struggled, the tighter he gripped, and I was shouting "Let go", swallowing water with each word. As I swallowed more of the pool, I recognized we were in serious danger. Now, I'm not sure that a ten-year old has much of a concept of death, and I certainly don't remember my life flashing before me, but

I do remember a kind of fear that came from some place so deep inside me that it surprised me. The one conscious thought that I recall clearly was that the lifeguards couldn't see us down here, and couldn't therefore save us. I felt responsible for my brother more than even being worried about myself. I think I uttered a prayer like, "Help us, God!" and the next thing I knew we were being propelled towards the surface so forcefully that we rose together high up out of the water and fell back down.

Tom let go of me as we broke the surface, but flailed wildly; and now that my arms were freed, I could try to get us over to the edge of the pool. I clutched him and swam clumsily, towing him to the side. We grabbed it together and hung on for dear life, our chests heaving as we gulped that precious air.

I remember tears streaming down my cheeks mixing with the chlorinated pool water, but don't remember now if they were tears of relief, happiness, or anger. Maybe some of all three… I don't think I did any heavy-duty introspection at that time, but do remember thinking back curiously to that sensation of being pushed by an unseen force to the surface of the water, and realizing that it wasn't by my doing that we were able to survive.

As I thought about ways that God may have acted in my life, I realized that other things that I had thought of as "lucky" may instead have been part of a pattern of intervention that protected me. At the age of two, I had swallowed an entire bottle of prescription cough syrup, and my mother had "luckily" come into the room in time to notice that the bottle had less in it than it should have, and was able to smell it on my mouth. She was, therefore, able to get me to the hospital in time to get my stomach pumped. When I was seven, I had walked alone to the airport in a fairly large city of 180,000 people to await the arrival of Roy Rogers because I had heard (by radio or word-of-mouth or something…) that he was coming into our airport. Unfortunately, I hadn't told anyone where I was going, and I waited most of the day to no avail. Now why didn't anyone at the airport wonder why a little girl was wandering around all day alone?

When I finally got back home (and to this day, I don't know how I really did it), my parents were hysterical with anxiety since I had been missing for twelve hours, but somehow I must have been walking with the angels because I was kept safe that whole time. Unfortunately, God apparently doesn't care to intervene when your parents want to punish you for scaring them half to death. These are certainly not huge or dramatic examples of heavenly aid, but because they happened to me, they have significance in my life.

I can think of many times that I felt "led" or "guided" to do things: entering the convent where I stayed happily for six years, going to live in Australia to teach school for two years, relocating to the opposite side of the country and being offered a job a week after I arrived, or leaving a secure, corporate job to do public speaking and training for large groups of sometimes hundreds of people. Many of these things I would not have envisioned myself doing, but simply followed the urgings of inspiration or worked with the opportunities as they presented themselves. In all of these situations, the circumstances led to wonderful experiences that have created a rich tapestry in my life, and chances to be of service to others.

Let me give an example of how fleeting and serendipitous some of these opportunities were. The move to Australia in 1974 was prompted by a "chance" meeting when a high school acquaintance came into the clothing store in Michigan where I worked in the evening as a second job. We chatted briefly about people we knew and she asked if I was aware that a mutual friend was teaching in Australia, and I replied that I wasn't. While she couldn't give me any specifics, it did inspire me to call the other friend's mother to see if she knew the name of a contact person who could give me some additional information.

The mother located the name of a professor at a university in California who did the recruiting for the Australian government and I sent off an air-mail letter, receiving a reply by return mail. I discovered that the recruiting team would be nearby—just 40 miles from my hometown in Michigan—for their semi-annual interviews 5 days later, and I obtained an appointment. The interview was successful, and two weeks after that I received a notice of acceptance requiring me to complete various formal documentation paperwork items and appear in Los Angeles for a flight to Sydney approximately one month later. I had first learned of the opportunity, followed up on it, successfully navigated the interview process, and completed endless paperwork to leave the country in less than 60 days. And what of the school acquaintance who just in passing in a "coincidental" five-minute meeting on a casual shopping trip had lighted this fire in me? I had not seen her since our graduation in the eight years prior to that encounter, and have never seen her again in the more than twenty years since...

Each of the examples I have mentioned above shows evidence in my life of a greater force at work than just chance or accidental circumstances. What I will attempt to explore through the hundreds of examples offered by the people in this book is the depth and richness of what is available to us to enhance our lives if we open our eyes and allow the possibility of an angel's hand taking ours. We will not be led wrong, but will discover exactly the right help, protection, or guidance to promote our best interests.

Angels Who Visit in Person

A Lesson in Trust

ROBABLY THE MOST STARTLING TYPE of angelic intervention comes in the form of a person who has offered aid or guidance to a human being. In the stories related to me where individuals believed they had interacted with a spiritual being in the form of a person, there is a dramatic and consistent occurrence. The angel takes on a form that is not frightening to the person or inappropriate to the circumstances. In fact, the physical appearance is something familiar or comforting or completely expected in that type of situation.

In the very first example, when Frank encounters a man in his living room, the stranger is dressed as a farmer and seems familiar, as if he is someone that knows Frank or knows the family. Since Frank had grown up on a farm in the "Pennsylvania Dutch" area of Pennsylvania, the "farmer appearance" would feel quite comfortable to him, whereas a quite different kind of apparition could have created such fear that perhaps the messenger and the message would both have been rejected. Although baffled by the experience, Frank paid attention to the message that was relayed, and trusted that the information was accurate. You will see how that affected his life.

In each of the stories in this section, the person involved must trust an apparition when he or she becomes a part of an unusual or a life-threatening situation. The almost miraculous nature of the outcome in many of the cases left an indelible stamp on the one who was helped, and many of them related that afterward their lives were never the same. Learning to trust someone or something that seems to defy the standard laws of nature can be difficult, and each of the individuals shown here had to momentarily suspend disbelief, or their desire for concrete proof, and simply let go and trust the "person" who came to help.

The first dramatic story involves a physical appearance of an angel offering a warning that ultimately saved a man's life.

Linda B., 43, Michigan, Automotive Industry
A visitor who appears unexpectedly warns a businessman to avoid an impending trip.

LINDA'S STORY IS ABOUT her now-deceased father, a wonderful man with whom she had a terrific relationship. One day her father, Frank, came home from work to an empty house where a very strange thing happened. He came out from the bathroom to find a man sitting in his living room! He described the man later as having the appearance of a farmer, the kind he had known as a youngster growing up in the Amish country of Pennsylvania. This man had a red beard, red hair, suspenders, loose overalls, and a worn cotton shirt.

Frank asked in a startled manner, "Who are you? What do you want?" "I have a message for you", the man replied quietly but firmly. "Tomorrow evening you must not fly your plane to Toledo." Now Frank was indeed a pilot who flew a small two-passenger aircraft as part of his business, and this message was quite disconcerting since he did have a meeting scheduled the following night when he and his partner (also a pilot) intended to fly to Toledo. He was still puzzled and ready to ask more questions when the man simply disappeared from the living room couch. One moment he was there, and the next, the room was empty.

Linda continued the story, "My father ran to the doors and checked, and they were all locked as they had been before. He thought maybe he had dreamed the encounter, but when he returned to the living room, it was still filled with the "presence" of this person who had seemed larger than life. Whenever he mentioned this to the family, he really had difficulty putting into words what this presence was. Usually he described it as an ultimate gentleness and peace, but always followed that with the statement that there were simply no words that could do it justice. His visitor absolutely radiated a sense of power and strength. My father went so far as to go outside to some neighbors who were standing in the street and ask "Did you see a man out here just now?" and described the individual of his encounter. Of course, their response was negative..."No Frank, there hasn't been anyone walking near your house in the last few minutes." So he went back inside, puzzled and incredulous.

He did, however, call his business partner and state that he did not want to fly to Toledo the following evening. Now his partner was not willing to take this at face value, and kept probing about my father's reason. Dad was somewhat reluctant to talk about his heavenly visitor (since he had by this time decided that he had no choice but to believe his eyes...he had seen and heard the man and then the man had disappeared into thin air...how else could this be explained?) and just said "someone told me not to go." His partner would not drop the issue, so Dad finally gave in and told him the story of his unexpected guest.

Dad's partner was quite skeptical, "C'mon Frank you don't buy into that do you? That's silly." But Dad couldn't shake the overwhelming feeling that he had to pay attention to this message, so he told his partner to go on to the meeting if he wanted to, but that Dad did not intend to go. It caused a few hard feelings between them at that point, but those feelings were later irrelevant when the following day's events occurred.

My father's partner insisted on going to the meeting in the company Cessna with another man, and the plane crashed before they arrived. The plane's two occupants were severely injured but ultimately survived, and Dad's partner always looked at him differently after that."

Linda said that it didn't give her father any pleasure to be right about the danger, but it did give him an extraordinary sense of being watched over and protected that he maintained until the day he died. "For the rest of his life, my father always had a kind of "special peace" that surrounded him, and he just didn't seem to be afraid of anything."

One of the incredible elements of this story is that the visitor appeared to Frank in a form that would not frighten him because of its familiarity. He told his family that the "countryish" look of the man was strangely comforting because it reminded him of the gentle old farmers that he had known and loved when he was growing up. It makes sense that an angel taking on a human form would certainly take care not to shock or frighten the person receiving the apparition because then the message could be lost as the person rejected the visitor.

Linda also described to me her father's wonder at the change in "atmosphere" in the house. When he went back into the house after checking outside to see where the stranger had disappeared, he still felt an "aura" of calm and peace in the living room. Even the air felt different. Frank had trouble putting into words the tremendous gentleness that emanated from his visitor—a kind of strength that felt limitless. He found that words did not come easily to describe the intensity of the sensations he had felt.

Linda had an experience of her own where she felt that a warning was given to her too. She was in Denver returning to Detroit and on the day of her scheduled flight she was plagued with a non-specific sense of apprehension that she just couldn't shake. Linda attributed this to normal "jitters" when you are out of your element and usual routine. However, as she was in line at the airport with her relative, the apprehension escalated to a sense of near terror and she felt strongly that she should not board the plane.

Voicing this fear was difficult because she feared her hosts would think she was quite strange, so she tried to think of excuses to delay her departure. Since they had an encouraging response for everything she suggested as reasons not to go, she finally had to confess. "I told them that I had an exceptionally strong feeling that I shouldn't go on that flight. They looked at me oddly but said they would support whatever I thought I needed to do and would be happy to take me back home with them if that's what I really wanted.

The plane that I had felt so strongly that I should avoid did indeed have mechanical problems on that exact flight, and ended up having to make a forced landing. Luckily no one was hurt, but it did give all the passengers a good scare, and I would have been one of them if I hadn't listened to that inner voice." Linda felt that she was far more sensitive to "messages" because of the many experiences that members of her family had had over the years.

Pastor Ed Glaspy, 47, Oregon, Director of the Restoration School
An athletic, young man appears to free a struggling driver trapped by a bus dashboard after an accident.

PASTOR ED PERFORMS his ministry at a three-month residence school for adult victims recovering from emotional or substance abuse trauma. Approximately 50 "students" at a time work on healing their lives and exploring the realities of a more spiritual existence.

In December 1989, Ed had been asked to drive a group of mostly high school and junior high students from the Christian school on a shopping trip to a large mall. The vehicle was an old commercial bus frequently used for transporting students. Heading into Eugene, they were following a semi truck that was filled with wood chips.

"I saw brake lights come on and I slowed down, but then the truck picked up speed again. The wood chip truck suddenly hit air brakes and had smoke emerging from it as it was required to stop fast. Unbeknownst to me, a 77 year-old man directly in front of the truck had started to pull off the road, but had apparently changed his mind and pulled back on right in front of the truck. It was in the brief second that I had glanced into my rear-view mirror to check vehicles around me that this truck had been required to slam on its brakes to avoid the older driver, but this had created a very dangerous situation for us. I stood on my brakes the best I could, but realized that I had absolutely no place to go.

We hit the truck! A loaded bus and a loaded chip truck do not make a good combination, even at 20 mph. Because the engine is in the back of this bus, there was no protection in front and the next thing I knew, I was being crushed in my seat by the dash and wheel that had been smashed inward by the force of the collision. I was pinned between the wheel and the seat and became aware of instant excruciating pain.

I pushed frantically but futilely on the twisted wheel, and prayed "Dear God, get me out of this." It seemed hopeless because the steering wheel seemed to touch the back of my seat, and no force could free me.

Suddenly a young man, who seemed to be in his 30s, appeared in front of me in the opening where, until moments ago, a windshield had been. He held onto the top of the bus, swung muscular legs through the opening, and pushed the back of the seat with his feet. I struggled out of the narrow gap, but was still trapped by the dash that was wrapped around my right foot. I spoke to my rescuer, "If you can push that again, I'll be able to squeeze my foot out." He did this for me and then moved around behind the driver's seat, and it was only later when I could process the whole experience piece by piece that I realized that there simply wasn't any place for him to be there, since there was no space behind the seat!

My rescuer put a hand on me, and I'll always remember the words he spoke: "Don't be afraid... everything will be alright." As I was checking on the others, I didn't immediately realize that I no longer saw that wonderful young man on the scene. I asked the principal, "Where is that young guy who pulled me out?" Steve looked quizzically, then doubtfully at me (perhaps fearing that I had suffered some kind of head injury) and said, "There wasn't anyone there. Do you mean the chip truck driver?" It was becoming more difficult to sort this out, so I decided to drop it at that point, and realized that since emergency personnel were arriving, my first priority was to survive. I would just have to sort it out later.

When they got me to the hospital, the situation was very serious and I was taken into surgery right away. It was devastating to realize that 80% of my large intestine had been pushed up into my stomach cavity, and the doctor informed me after the surgery that most of the actual intestines had disintegrated, his expression was "they had exploded." That meant there was a potential for a tremendous amount of infection. The strangest part of all was hearing the doctor say that when they performed surgery, they found an imprint of a steering wheel on the inside of my back. He had used massive amounts of some solution to cleanse as much of my insides as he could get to. When I came out of the operation, I found myself with a colostomy bag and a serious situation, but I never became discouraged.

The doctors were amazed at how fast I recovered, but I know that it was because I was in the presence of the Lord the whole time. I'm certain that people will think that this is a strange thing for me to say, but the entire period I was in the hospital was a truly glorious time for me. One night when my wife and friends were visiting, we were reliving the day of the accident, and I mentioned that I really wanted to find the person who had helped me so I could thank him.

After everyone left, I was praying and God started running pictures through my mind of all the near accidents I had had in my life. It was like watching a movie except that I was the star of every scene, and each one triggered a memory. In the last accident scene, I saw the rear of the chip truck coming toward me, and suddenly there was the face of the young man who had rescued me. I felt more than heard God say, "That is the face of your angel..."

Now this reinforced for me what I had begun to believe: that I had been visited by an angel. I had initially thought of this when just two people on that bus, one teacher and one student, had both related perfectly how I had been pulled from the crushed seat, and both described the muscular stranger. It was comforting to me that someone else had seen exactly what I had seen; that validation was really important to me. All of the others, however, had seen no one.

I want to revisit why I felt so strongly that my hospital stay was a blessed time. For one, I knew God was healing me. Sometimes when I was praying, I could see a light shining on my abdomen or other parts of my body, and I knew it was working a healing miracle.

I was home for Christmas Day. Just ten days after the accident, I had my first small meal of any substance and shared it with my family, despite being the patient whose doctor had said that he had *never* seen such serious trauma to the intestines! All I know for sure is that my sense of God's peace never deserted me. And the certainty of knowing that I have that guardian angel with me is comforting when moments of danger are around."

Anyone wishing more information about the Restoration School at the Christ Center can locate Pastor Ed Glaspy in Junction City, Oregon.

*   *   *

In the next story about Toni, the person she meets has a very disgusting appearance but influences her to change her life in dramatic ways. It may be difficult to believe that an angel would assume such a revolting form, but it cannot be denied that some kind of special interaction occurred. This situation could be one where an angelic being appeared to guide her or it could simply be an encounter of two humans, but one in which the circumstances were somehow altered to inspire Toni's change of heart. You decide.

Toni L., 46, Arizona, User Support Documentation Trainer
A stranger with a heavenly voice teaches Toni to trust inner guidance again.

TONI FEELS SINGULARLY BLESSED to be at the point in her life where she is. A survivor of childhood abuse that left her an emotional wasteland for years, she is currently traveling a path of constant growth that challenges her daily to be more than an oblivious wanderer on the path of life. Toni speaks of tuning in to 'quiet places' during a busy day where a silent voice speaks to her inside teaching, leading, guiding, helping..."There is so much external stimuli in our daily lives, we get so busy about terribly mundane things that we forget to listen to what's inside."

Toni lives a life that is more consciously aware of what happens around her than most people are. She has learned to listen for soft messages that come unbidden to lead her along a particular path; sometimes these "urgings" are so strong that she feels compelled to act on something where she isn't even certain what the result will be. But still she follows that guiding hand... Toni attributes her current awareness to an experience more than six years ago that still moves her to tears of wonderment at the recollection.

"I was on my way to a ballgame with a friend when we passed a Circle K across from the park. Sitting out under a light in the parking lot was an obvious transient who was one of the truly filthiest people I have ever seen. It is hard to find words to describe the degree of dirtiness I witnessed: matted hair and decrepit clothing doesn't even begin to communicate his appearance. I know that in my thoughts there was a kind of "instant awareness" of his presence. My friend and I continued to our game, and as we later left, I saw this same man now lying in the center of the park.

An internal urging started that slowly grew stronger and stronger as I got nearer to my home. Without understanding why, I was experiencing an intense desire to do something to help this man, so I said to my friend, "Say a little prayer for my safety because I'm going to take some things to that man we saw in the park." My friend, of course, was astonished and tried to urge me to rethink this rash action. This man could be a drug addict, be in an alcoholic stupor that could turn ugly, could pull out a weapon and threaten or harm me. Great! All I needed was something else to be fearful of.

What you need to know is that at this point in my life, I was dealing heavily with issues about trust and faith that had come from my terrible background. I was having difficulty trusting anyone, but there simply wasn't any denying this compelling inner 'pushing.' Despite my friend's cautions, I put some food and a blanket and pillow into a bag and set out for the park where I had last seen the man. I was actually making "bargains" with God…I would only go if it was not too dark so I wouldn't be terrified…but it couldn't be so light that people would know who I was…among other equally odd requirements. They sound a little silly now, but seemed to make sense at the time. Actually, I was absolutely terrified, and couldn't believe my feet were indeed carrying me out into the night, alone, on this seemingly irrational errand of mercy.

How unlike me this was. Despite the wildly fluttering butterflies, I arrived at the park and saw the man exactly as I had viewed him earlier, covered with a tarp. I ventured, "Excuse me, but I brought you some things…" He lifted the edge of the tarp so I could see him, and shocked me when he spoke with the most indescribably beautiful and melodious voice, "What is your name?" I could barely croak, "...Toni" —that unbelievable voice had literally taken my breath away. He was so incredibly articulate, literate, educated, seemingly a world away from the degradation he represented as someone rootless, alone, not meeting the barest necessities of life.

Again the resonant, harmonious sound that reached deep into my soul, "Thank you Toni." I longed to hear him continue that beautiful, lyrical timbre that seemed to drift into the air and float away as delicate as a caress. I was so totally enveloped by this man's presence that as I turned to leave, the feeling of parting with something sweet and precious was almost tangible. His voice had erased the dirt, the matted hair, and the ugliness that his condition represented.

I looked for that man the next day, but (not really a surprise to me) he wasn't there; I had never seen him before and I have never seen him since. Looking back with only the kind of perspective that time can offer, I honestly believe I saw an angel in the flesh in the most unlikely of appearances, the most repulsive of disguises, but one that was meant to teach me a critical life lesson. I learned about trusting the guidance you receive, not letting your fears cripple you into inaction, but to step out into unfamiliar territory and reach out to others.

Somehow, and I'm not sure how I heard or knew this, I know his name was Arthur. The incredible presence that this man had affects me to this day because whenever I think about it now, a place inside me opens up and something sweet washes through me in a kind of internal rebirth. When I speak of this experience today, it is as real to me as if it has just happened, and I am reminded anew of how blessed I was. On that dark evening in a park six years ago, I started to live again."

Leslie F., 41, California, Systems Software Specialist
Leslie's story is very special because she was an innocent nine year-old when her life could have

been snuffed out by a cold, unforgiving lake. Her rescuer makes sure that Leslie has another chance.

ANGELS ARE NEARBY WHEN CHILDREN ARE ALONE, and the one who came to rescue Leslie was quite special indeed. When she was 11 years old, Leslie and a small group of four or five friends and siblings were playing at Freshwater Pool, a recreation site near Eureka, California. This is a natural stream that feeds into a man-made pool, and the youngsters were in the water without any adult supervision and without any other visitors present while they were there.

The rambunctious children had created a wild game with a raft—all the kids would pile onto one side of the raft, tipping it precariously while the last child was responsible for holding it as long as possible before letting go with a force that would catapult the rest across the water. When Leslie's turn to hold the raft came, as the children soared away, it overturned trapping her underneath.

By the time the others noticed that they couldn't see her, she had swallowed a tremendous amount of water and after gasping valiantly for a last few desperate breaths of air was sinking rapidly for the second and probably final time. The other children were too far away to swim back to help and everyone, even Leslie herself, realized with horror that she might truly drown.

As Leslie relates, "I was flailing helplessly and sinking fast and was absolutely terrified. Suddenly, I found myself grasped firmly around the waist by strong hands and was propelled upwards toward that sweet, fresh air. Gasping and choking, I was carried toward the shore by a man dressed in a wetsuit and a face mask but without any kind of airtank. He never said a word to me except "You can stand up here" as we reached the shallow part of the shoreline.

The reassuring hands let go and my rescuer simply walked away from me out of the water toward the parking area and just disappeared. My friends swam up filled with questions, all talking at once, "Who was that?", "Where did that man come from, there's not even a car parked anywhere", "We've been here for over three hours and haven't seen ANYONE, not even the caretaker, where has that man been?" They scanned the empty parking area. All of the youngsters had seen the diver, but not one of them saw where he went, despite the several sets of eyes that had watched the rescue. The mysterious diver (with no air supply) seemed to have vanished into thin air."

When asked how this incident had affected her life, Leslie replied, "I began to believe that there was a special purpose for my life, and I was on earth to make some kind of contribution. What I do today to act on that is to devote my career to service—I work in a scripture-based recovery program that is like a 12-step program, and I have been doing that for about five years.

I have seen miracles happen for people, many have regained self-esteem and a sense of mission where they previously had despair and aimlessness. They truly begin to live. Does it matter to the world that I am here to do this? I think the answer is Yes."

Joe Y., 59, Arizona, Budget Analyst
Joe trusts the vision of a helpful guide that prevents him from crashing his car when he falls asleep at the wheel.

"WHILE I WAS STATIONED AT AN AIRBASE in Mississippi in 1953, I was traveling home to Idaho for Christmas with several of my buddies. We had taken turns driving for two solid days so that we could go straight through and have more time to spend with our families. As we got to within about ten miles of our destination, we encountered a horrible accident and felt so sorry for whoever was involved because that would be awful at the holidays. We all noticed a young Marine sergeant directing traffic around the accident, but didn't think anything about it, just assumed that he was a kindhearted passerby who had stopped to help. He didn't seem out of the ordinary, but simply another military person like us who was heading home for the holiday.

Two nights later, I encountered this person again, but in the most unusual of circumstances. I had asked a girlfriend out to the movies that night but I was very, very tired and I fell asleep at the wheel of my car on the way home. The Marine sergeant I had seen a few days before appeared in a dream and directed me where to drive my car. I know this sounds really weird, but he was motioning me where to go and I followed the directions which placed me onto a bridge and prevented me from driving into a canal.

My girlfriend was startled because she didn't understand where I was going, and then she realized I wasn't responding to her and woke me up. I mentioned the Marine to her and she didn't know what I was talking about because she hadn't seen anything.

There doesn't seem to be any kind of logical explanation for the incidents I'm describing, so I have always felt that something really unusual had happened that maybe could only be understood by a leap of faith. All my life since then, I've believed that I was helped in some spiritual way, and have tried to live up to the responsibility of that by trying to help others."

Halli M., 36, Oregon, Mental Health Agency
Both Halli and her mother trust the people who come to help when they are filled with doubt and fear. The peace and strength that their messengers bring is a priceless gift.

"MY FATHER WAS IN THE HOSPITAL for surgery on a very large mass and the growth was a terrible concern for the family because we were fearful that it was cancer. In the hospital, the night before the surgery, my mother was sitting silently beside my father's bed as he dozed. When a woman in white entered and came to her side, my mother assumed that it was a nurse. The woman spoke to her and said, "Don't worry about your husband any further. This is cancer, but it is contained within a cyst and he will recover."

My mother was greatly relieved and shared this with us in the morning, but I became quite upset and thought, "How dare someone say that to her when he hasn't even had the surgery yet. How could they even know?" My mother seemed somewhat puzzled and confused when I asked her about this, and hadn't thought to ask further about who was giving her this information. I, however, decided in a fit of righteous indignation, that I would track down the culprit and give this person a piece of my mind.

I set out to find the mysterious informant, but the hospital said that no one who was on the shift the previous evening had spoken to my mother. Now this was very curious, so I asked them to check again. The same result occurred…there was no staff person of the description provided by my mother, and no one admitted to comforting her.

When my father had his surgery that day, the prediction came true. The mass indeed was cancerous, but had been caught just prior to breaking through the wall of the cyst, so all of the cancer was removed and my father did recover.

We all felt after this experience that somehow we might have been the receivers of a very special visitation. There didn't appear to be any other explanation for someone who could know the outcome ahead of time since no medical staff member could give that kind of advice. We felt very blessed for my father's fortunate recovery."

"On one other occasion, I had a very strange experience that left me wondering if I hadn't personally received some heavenly help in escaping a dangerous situation. When I lived in Colorado, I was caught in an exceptionally bad ice and snow storm. Since I had no chains on my car, I was fearful about getting home but only had about twelve miles to travel. After discussing this by telephone with my husband, I agreed to try to get home, but simply to turn around if I ran into trouble.

It was awful to see stranded vehicles scattered every few feet along the roadway, but slowly I crept along successfully negotiating one slick hill after another. I prayed throughout, asking God to stay with me and get me home. As I came to one of the last steep hills near our house, I thought, "If I can make it up just this one last obstacle, I'll be home free." I felt a little elation as I realized I was almost safe.

Suddenly, about halfway up the hill, my car skidded to a halt and tires spun as I couldn't get it to go further…I was stranded halfway up the slope. My heart almost stopped I was so afraid…here it was, pitch dark, no one around, almost 1 a.m., freezing cold. I thought that I too would have to abandon my car and try to hike home down dark streets. Should I sit there and keep trying to get my car to inch upward and then slip back?

Wearily, I put my head down on the steering wheel and prayed a heartfelt prayer, "Oh God, help me now, give me the strength to get home." At that moment, a tap sounded near my ear stirring me from my thoughts, and I looked up to see a figure outlined in that frost-clouded window. I felt relief flooding through me as I put the window down. It was absolutely the tallest policewoman I had ever seen, and she was asking if she could help me.

I nearly wept with joy as I told her what had happened and she offered to push me up the hill and get me home. With that I realized that there were bright lights in my mirror, and it was only later that I stopped to wonder how they had got there when the last thing I remember was being alone on a dark street. At that moment I was too relieved to question anything.

True to her word, my helper returned to her vehicle and with a slight bump we started moving slowly up the hill. Finally, we reached the top, and she got out of her car to come back up to my window. She told me which streets to take to get home safely, and then simply drove off. I was never in a position to see what type of car she was in, and didn't even get a good look at her uniform under the heavy jacket, I only know it seemed official.

As she promised, I arrived home after just another few minutes and was ecstatic to be back with my family. It was only later that the nagging questions arose: How could she be there so quickly when I had thought there was no one around on that street? Had I prayed with my eyes closed longer than I thought? And why would she push me when police usually just radio for a tow truck or some other emergency vehicle? Because she thought all the trucks would be busy? And probably the question that became the biggest one of all...How could she start from a stopped position and have the "oomph" to not only get her own car to go upward on an icy surface, but to have the ability to push my car from a dead stop too? That seemed the most impossible feat of all.

While I am perfectly willing to believe that this was only a human police officer after all, who happened to be in the right place at the right time to aid me, I am also willing to believe that God sent a heavenly helper to get me home when nothing else was available on a human level. The officer drove away so quickly that I didn't have a chance to check out anything that could have told me where that car originated, but I'm grateful if it was indeed an angelic officer."

Terri S., 33, Arizona, Civil Engineering
An "encyclopedia salesperson" with the kindest and most gentle demeanor renews Terri's hope just when her world seems darkest.

"IN 1991, I WAS IN A VERY DEPRESSED PERIOD of my life, probably one of the worst times I have ever been through. Although I was raising small children, I had asked my husband to leave our house, and found myself in absolutely dire straits to the point of expecting my electricity to be turned off at any time.

One day, a man selling encyclopedias came to my door. I told him with tears springing to my eyes that I couldn't even consider looking at his books since I couldn't afford to put food on my table, not even macaroni and cheese. This man had the most wonderfully warm, deep eyes and looked at me with such caring and compassion that I just let go and sobbed wildly as I told him what was happening in my life. I told him how hopeless I felt and how worried I was about my little ones. He just enfolded me with his concern and I felt that he understood what I was saying at a level I couldn't even express.

This "salesperson" then took me outside into the carport, held my hand with great tenderness, and prayed out loud with me. He told me that I must forgive anyone who I felt had harmed me and let go of the pain and sadness. I did this with a sense of a burden being lifted away from me, although I wasn't sure exactly what it was. When we were through, this kind stranger looked deep into my eyes (and my heart, I think...), handed me $80 out of his pocket, and said "God bless you". He then turned and walked toward the driveway.

I started into the house, and then suddenly turned to wish my visitor a pleasant day, and to thank him once more, but the driveway was curiously empty. How could he have walked out of my sight in just a matter of seconds? Puzzled, I walked out onto the street, but saw nothing, no salesman, no car, nothing. Thinking he may have walked faster than I realized and may have been in a neighbor's house already (even as I tried weakly to convince myself this was feasible, my mind was rejecting this amazing feat as physically impossible), I stood on the sidewalk for a full half hour waiting for him to reappear from a nearby house. Of course he didn't.

I struggled to accept the enormity of what had happened because I was suddenly convinced beyond any doubt that I had been visited by an angel of God. My mind boggled...why should I have been so blessed? In the end, all I could do was accept this gift and use the strength and energy I felt flowing from this to enrich my interactions with others."

Cindy G., 38, California, Computer Industry
A stranger helps when a frightened woman's car breaks down.

"IN 1992, I WAS TRAVELING ON I-680 going toward Redding, California when my car overheated and I was forced to stop in a pretty barren area at a small, seedy gas station. I was waiting for my car to cool down and just idly passing time when a man started hanging around near me and finally spoke, "You're not from around here are you?" The eerie, predatory look in his eyes terrified me more than the leering tone in his voice.

I couldn't wait to get out of there and finally left. As I was passing over the Benicia Bridge, the engine light came on again and the car appeared to be overheating once more, except this area was even less inhabited than the first one. I will admit to being very scared because I was alone and had to pull over in a gravel area about 6 p.m. No one stopped to help me, and I began to cry, praying for some kind of help.

Suddenly, a white car was sitting there and a very nice-looking man was climbing out. He wore all white—white jeans, white shirt, and he had the most beautiful blue eyes. The strange thing was that I had not heard the car pull up and I was in a position to hear any vehicle approaching me. I had really only taken my eyes off the road for a second. "Can I help you?" the stranger asked kindly. I explained my predicament to him and he said, "Would you like to use the phone right here?" He pointed toward an emergency phone which was about 10 feet away, so I called for the AAA road service and ordered a tow truck. In my confused condition I had not even seen the phone!

He offered to wait with me for awhile, and I was grateful for the company when a scruffy-looking person pulled up in a red truck and was trying to get me to leave with him. The stranger with me said firmly, "No. She has help coming. She's fine." That discouraged the other man so he finally left. My friend in white offered to wait longer with me, but I was reluctant to inconvenience him, so I said I would be O.K. I remember him telling me that I should get in my car and lock the door and I would be just fine. He turned to leave and I began to walk toward my car. At that point, I noticed how dark it had become and thought maybe it would be better to have company after all. So I spun on my heel to catch him and tell him that I would appreciate his companionship after all until the tow truck came, and he had vanished, car and all! There were no tire tracks in the gravel and I had not heard the sound of a car driving away. He would not have had enough time to get to his car and get it started anyway.

Right then, I suspected that maybe an angel had stopped by to strengthen me, and somehow it was as if he had stayed anyway because I had a calm, strong sense that I would be fine, and I was."

Mary L., 52, Missouri, Federal Agency
Mary learns of a man whose arms are fifteen feet wide who is present in her husband's hospital room as he faces almost certain death.

IN 1985, MARY'S HUSBAND had a massive heart attack at the age of 47, and had only a 1% chance of survival according to the doctors who treated him. He was in a coma for four days, and as he related to her later, during that time he could simultaneously see himself lying on the hospital bed and sitting in a beautiful countryside feeling very peaceful. The most interesting occurrence happened as he emerged from the coma.

Mary says, "He told me that he was tapped on the head by a person he saw as he came to consciousness. I was not in the room at that second, but came in just a few minutes later. He told me that he had seen a huge shining man whose outstretched hands extended from the door on one side to the window on the other. In the room he was in, that was a distance of about 15 feet so that would have been one huge person.

He was certain that this man had awakened him and he told me about this very excitedly. What is very odd is that after he told me about it, the memory seemed to be gone. I asked him about his mysterious huge man one time after that and he didn't know what I was talking about. I found that very curious. He later had an operation that removed 30% of his heart.

The most interesting thing is the reactions of people such as his doctors and his parish priest. The doctors said that no other patient at Barnes Hospital had ever survived this particular type of heart attack. Even if he did, they expected he would be on oxygen for the rest of his life, which he wasn't.

His parish priest had said, "People can think whatever they want about this, but I can come up with no other explanation than that it was a miracle."

My husband himself seemed to have a newfound peace. At the time of his heart attack, he seemed to be very afraid of dying, and he has since told me many times that death holds no terror for him and he can leave this earth easily when he is supposed to. For me, that is one of the most startling revelations of all, because I know how fearful he had been.

This entire unfolding of events has truly strengthened our faith and hope, and made us a much more loving and dedicated family. Although my husband now has no memory of the man he encountered in his hospital room so many years ago, I believe that it was an angel that stood so protectively at his bedside, and that this angel has been present to keep him going ever since. We feel very blessed."

Pat S., Oklahoma, Administrative Secretary
Who were those unusual hitchhikers on the freeway?

"I HAVE A FRIEND WHO experienced an unusual situation in which he was driving on the Interstate, a natural part of his job since he was in a traveling sales position. He had an ironclad policy to never pick up hitchhikers, but when he saw two men in business suits walking on the side of the road one day, he assumed that their car had broken down even though he didn't see a vehicle stranded anywhere. He stopped and offered the men a ride even as he wondered momentarily why he was breaking his own rule not to pick people up.

One hitchhiker got into the front and one got into the back, and my friend greatly enjoyed visiting with them since the time passed quickly. At one point they asked to be dropped off at an interchange, which my friend agreed to do, and he wished them a pleasant goodbye. As he drove away, he glanced into his rear-view mirror and was surprised to see that they were gone since they had not had time to walk anywhere else. He drove slowly for a few minutes, craning his neck to see in every direction, but there was no sign of his companions. They had simply disappeared.

When he stopped briefly at the next town for gas, there was a buzz of apprehension among the residents about an escaped murderer at-large in the very area he had just passed through. My friend could not help but wonder if his companions had been more than just plain hitchhikers and in some way perhaps had protected him from harm even though he had not seen any sign of the escapee."

SOME PEOPLE HAVE PERCEIVED THEIR HELPERS IN UNIQUE FORMS

Lisa L., 26, Minnesota, Developmental Disability Agency
Where did the mysterious dog come from?

"I HAVE A FRIEND WHO WAS home alone while his wife and two-month old baby were visiting friends out of town. Now you need to understand that this man was in perfect health. Suddenly he felt his right side go numb, and when he went into the bathroom to revive himself, he collapsed.

He was found the next day after someone in his apartment building came over to see why he didn't answer the phone. When they got him to the hospital, the prognosis was quite grim—his doctors were saying there would be no recovery and he would probably be in a vegetative state and would not return to any kind of normal functioning.

They did perform surgery on him and he regained consciousness. After the surgery, he kept asking his wife, "Where's the dog?", and Natalie would continually reply, "Honey, we don't have a dog, remember?" They all felt that it was some kind of delusion he was suffering from because of the trauma of the stroke.

But her husband swore that all the time he was in the bathroom he was given companionship by a german shepherd who kept him awake as much as possible, kept him warm, licked him and told him everything would be alright. He wasn't sure if he actually heard the words or felt them in some kind of telepathic way, but he is certain that there was some form of communication that passed between them.

My friend then experienced an almost miraculous, complete recovery, and returned to perfect health in less than two months. He certainly astonished all those who thought he would be vegetative."

Shawn M., 34, Arizona, Sanitation Supervisor

A rabbit suddenly signals the dangerous, imminent end of a road. Without that, would Shawn's motorcycle have gone out of control?

SHAWN REMEMBERS AN UNUSUAL visitation at the age of 18 that saved him from a potentially serious accident with a motorcycle. He had experience riding cycles for approximately two years, when he was returning home very late one evening down an unfamiliar road. He thought it would be a shortcut even though he had never traveled this way and didn't know exactly where it went.

Abruptly, a jackrabbit darted across the road in front of him. While it posed no danger to him, Shawn said it prompted a series of "microsecond" thoughts: "Rabbit…desert, desert…road ends…, road ends…brake" which he promptly did. "I was going about 35 mph at that moment and I didn't brake a second too soon. Maybe 50 feet farther, the road stopped and no sign had been posted anywhere to say that!

There was a dropoff of 24 inches or so, and when I dropped off the end of the road, because I had braked so sharply I was only going 15-20 mph and had no problem controlling the bike. If I had flown over the dropoff at 35 mph, I would have been badly injured or killed because I wouldn't have been able to stabilize the motorcycle; it most certainly would have gone out of control.

At the time, I just thought "What a lucky thing that rabbit ran out." But as I got older I began to wonder if that wasn't a very specific warning meant to help me. I guess what also made me look deeper is hearing about things that happened to others after that and knowing what happened to me later.

I was at a traffic light once and it turned green, but the person next to me didn't move. I pivoted to see why he wasn't starting up and took a minute to admire his neat Jaguar. As I twisted back and we both began moving, some car ran the red light at about 75 mph right in front of us. It passed us by a hair's breadth and I realized that if we had started our cars up when the light changed we both would have been pancakes.

What caused us both to wait? A friend in Long Island, New York was also first in line at an intersection when his car died and he couldn't get it started as the light changed. He was grinding away at the ignition, pretty annoyed, when the car that went past beside him in the next lane at full speed was in a serious accident in the middle of the intersection right in front of him. The sobering thought in each case was "one second more and it would have been me."

From the time these things happened to me, I have lived my life trying to make a contribution because clearly there is a reason for what happened."

Kay O., 62, Minnesota, Non-Profit Agency
The spider who saved the baby.

"SOMETHING HAPPENED TO ME in 1936 when I was only 3 years old and living in Baltimore. I had been left in the care of a babysitter while my mother was at work, and when I fell asleep, the sitter had left the bedlight burning to keep me company. I felt a "daddy longlegs" stroking my forehead which woke me up, and when I saw the spider, I screamed and jumped to the end of the bed. My screams alerted the babysitter who rushed into the room and found the pillow on fire where the bedlamp had fallen onto the linens.

She was able to put the fire out immediately. Without that spider startling me, I probably would have burned to death because the babysitter would never have discovered the fire in time to save me."

LESSONS IN TRUST

Each of the stories in this chapter required the person involved to simply trust the help received whether or not it seemed to come the way he or she thought it would. We can learn valuable lessons from paying attention to the ways in which we are assisted.

1. Help can come from an unexpected source.

2. The external, visible signs and symbols in our experiences are not always the most significant. If we listen to our underlying feelings and thoughts, they are often more accurate.

3. We are each truly deserving to be the recipient of a wondrous encounter. It is not "something that happens to other people, but could never happen to me..."

4. Gratitude is important. These encounters are very special gifts for our welfare.

5. We each need to be more observant in ordinary events of our lives to be open to the miraculous.

6. Our angels, guides, and teachers are always there, ready and willing to assist, but we must usually ASK them to perform this task. They will not be intrusive into a human life.

7. We need to be aware that unusual forms for our helper may be acceptable, such as our perception of animals coming to our aid.

PERSONAL JOURNAL

Ask yourself the following questions and write down significant thoughts and feelings:

1. Have I ever been in a situation where I was aware that I was specifically receiving help from a source beyond normal human experience? What happened?

2. Did I trust what was happening or did I doubt the experience?

3. What outcome resulted that in some way affected my life? Was this a short-term or long-term outcome?

4. Have I shared this experience with other people?

5. How could I be more conscious of the possibility of interacting with an angel or guide?

INDIVIDUAL INSIGHTS AND OBSERVATIONS
ABOUT "TRUST" IN MY LIFE:

Write in a journal any thoughts that come to mind.

Angels Who Offer Helping Hands

A Lesson in Wonder

T HE "HANDS" OF ANGELS are what sometimes offer us the greatest gift. Those moments when we cannot do something for ourselves are the very times when our helpers and guardians are most in evidence.

The stories described in this section all involve some kind of intervention where a person has been in dire need of assistance, has been unable to act alone, or has been physically incapable of accomplishing whatever was needed to escape from or resolve a situation. Many of the examples that were told to me seem to be small miracles because they defy logical and rational explanation. In each case, however, a human being was left better off for the extension of a heavenly hand, and a stronger and deeper faith invariably resulted.

A majority of the people specifically talked about the presence of a "hand" that in some way touched them by such means as turning on a hospital call light, pulling a cord from an outlet that was causing an electrocution, holding a young man falling from a "cherry-picker", picking up a monstrous tree, guiding the steering wheels of cars, and pulling victims from crashed automobiles.

Sally W., 55, Kansas, Pharmaceuticals
A sleeping patient in imminent danger is rescued by an unseen hand.

"TWENTY-FIVE YEARS AGO, I was hospitalized just before the birth of my child because I had started to hemmorhage severely and they felt the baby was in danger. I was supposed to be stabilized overnight before they did a sonogram (this was a very new, almost experimental procedure at this time) in the morning, and then the doctor intended to induce labor or perform a Caesarean section.

I was sleeping on my side facing the wall where the doorway opened onto the hall. I awoke from what felt like a very deep sleep to see a nurse standing in the doorway. She turned away and ran down the hall, apparently summoning help from other staff members, because the next thing I knew, several people were racing into the room, swarming around my bed and lifting me onto a gurney. Although I was feeling a little "fuzzy", as they moved me away from the bed I had been sleeping in, I was horrified to see a huge and spreading pool of blood. How could that be when I wasn't feeling any pain? Shouldn't I hurt somewhere?

They sped me through the hushed and darkened hallways to an operating room where the staff finally got things under control. By the time it was over, I had lost my son as well as five units of blood, but they told me I had almost lost my life too. Apparently, it was a real miracle that I came through.

I spoke to my nurse later and asked, "They told me that there were only moments between life and death last night. What brought you into my room just in time to get me into surgery? Did I scream or cry out?" She looked at me curiously and said, "You put your call light on for me. Don't you remember? I came because you called me."

Now that really shook me, because I knew for a fact I did *not* put that light on, and I doubt very much if my hand accidentally found and pressed that tiny button while I was sound asleep. *To this day, I am convinced that a guardian angel turned that light on to help me.* I have always felt special since then and believed that there was a definite purpose to my life. I have treasured every experience that has happened to me and tried to live my life in a way that it would make some contribution back to the world. It is the most wonderful and comforting and amazing thing to know for a fact that you were touched by an angel."

Jim B., 36, Indiana, Manufacturing Warehouse

A young warehouse worker is ready to fall over twenty feet onto a concrete floor when a hand is felt in the middle of his back...

"IN 1978, I WAS WORKING IN A WAREHOUSE Receiving Department at a factory when I needed to get a small motor off the top shelf of a very high rack. I had to use a "cherry-picker" for the task, and that piece of equipment has one ironclad safety rule: Always put the guardrail down when you have to go up in the air.

Now this particular time, I didn't bother to put the guardrail in place because I was thinking, "This is just a quick task, it will only take a minute and I'll be right back down..." I went up about 22 feet above the concrete floor, reached out and grabbed the handle of the cardboard crate that contained the motor I needed. The cardboard ripped and the momentum caused me to topple backwards through the opening where the guardrail should have been positioned to save me.

Because I had neglected to follow one simple safety procedure, my life was now threatened.

As I fell backwards, *I felt the pressure of a strong, firm hand placed squarely in the middle of my back holding me and preventing me from falling to the unyielding floor below.* It may sound strange, but I know at that moment I had a guardian angel taking care of me and I wasn't even afraid, although I should have been terrified. To this day, years later, I can still remember the feeling of that gentle yet solid touch that saved my life. I feel too, that my faith has deepened throughout my life since then and has been a source of tremendous strength for me."

Frank S., 65, Michigan, Retired clothing store owner
A father struggles to free his son who is trapped beneath a huge tree, but he cannot do it alone...

"MY FRIEND FLOYD, who was in his middle sixties when this happened, bought a farm near Coopersville, and had to go cut down a huge old dead tree on his new property. His son, who was then in his late twenties, went to help him with this task when a terrible thing happened. The tree twisted unexpectedly and fell trapping his son underneath, badly mangling the son's leg. Floyd *picked up the huge tree and moved it* so that his son could free his leg, but the young man found the leg was useless and he could not put any weight on it or walk on it.

Frantically, Floyd picked up his son, a man who weighed about 200 pounds, and carried him almost an eighth of a mile to the truck they had taken to the job-site. By getting his son to the hospital in time for treatment to save the leg, Floyd accomplished something that he later decided was a small miracle.

When they returned to finish the job of removing the dead tree, Floyd tried to shift the tree and discovered that he could not in any way budge or move the huge trunk even one-half inch on his own, much less lift it into the air. He also tried to pick up his son and found that he couldn't carry him more than two feet without dropping him. The tremendous strength that he had in a moment of extreme fear for his son's welfare almost had to come from some outside source. Floyd felt he had received special help at a dangerous time."

Anita T., 26, New Mexico, Federal Government Agency

An angel hand pulls a cord from an electrical outlet just in time to save a young man.

"MY UNCLE WAS WORKING ALONE very late one night in his auto body shop, and he was using an electrical sander to sand a fender. While he was working, the place where the sander cord and the extension cord were connected happened to hit a puddle and he was being electrocuted. As he was shaking and frozen in one position, he happened to be facing the wall where the outlet was, and *he distinctly saw the plug pull out of the wall socket and drop to the floor,* stopping the flow of current that was paralyzing him.

My brother knows that he could not have pulled on it, because the cord was looped and had slack in it; in fact it was that slack part that had passed through the puddle of water. He recovered just fine, but absolutely believes that there was an angel present who saved him from death."

Michele A., 27, California, Legal Industry

Gentle arms lift a teenager through the window of a car during a rollover accident.

"WHEN I WAS JUST 18 YEARS OLD, I was driving with my boyfriend to an old country store in Kentucky during the late afternoon, when a cat ran out in front of our car. He swerved and the vehicle overturned, rolling several times. The most incredible thing happened while the car was in the middle of the rolling before it stopped. *I definitely felt like there were strong arms picking me up underneath my armpits, and I was pulled through the open window.* I felt my stomach and my leg scrape against the edge of the window, and the feeling was distinctly one of being dragged.

This was such a mind-boggling thing that I could barely comprehend what was happening when I found myself standing upright on the sidewalk! As I stared in a daze at the overturned car, my boyfriend and another friend of his were slowly struggling out the open but dented window. Someone was certainly taking care of me! In addition to whatever angels watch over us, I have always felt very close to my great-grandmother and feel that she is somehow also near when I need her."

David S., 33, California, Hotel Supervisor
A mother's hasty prayer sends an angel to her son's side.

"IN 1979, I WAS WORKING AS A FIREFIGHTER and was going to a party with a friend on his Harley, and told my mother shortly before we left. Probably less than 30 minutes after that, she heard my "Plectron" go off (a transmitter that identifies the address of an emergency since I was often on call), and she told me later that a sudden chill went through her and she just knew with a terrible sense of foreboding that it was me. She checked the transmitter for the address and went to the scene, finding to her dismay that she was right, and I was indeed a victim of an accident.

The strange part of this story is that while I had suffered negligible damage— a scrape on my hand—my friend who was driving the Harley was severely injured. The doctors on this case stated that they found it hard to believe that the two of us had been in the same accident.

My mother told me that when I had mentioned the party, she had uttered a brief prayer for the angels to go with me and take care of me. The weird thing is that when the impact occurred, I had felt almost as if I was being lifted up by some kind of huge, strong hand. The lack of injury seems to speak for itself that someone was helping me, so do I believe in angels? Absolutely!"

Sue S., 44, Wisconsin, Sales Administration

Sue's car is steered safely when she falls asleep at the wheel.

"I HAVE EXPERIENCED A QUITE unusual kind of helping hand that I have never been able to duplicate. In 1993, I spent many of my evenings going to school to improve my education while also working at a full-time and a part-time job. This was truly exhausting for me and sometimes it seemed more than I could handle to just keep juggling all those activities.

One day I was on my way to school about 4:30 in the afternoon and simply fell asleep at the wheel of my car. A jerk of my steering wheel awoke me; *it was turning, but I had not done it.* In fact, it was the weirdest feeling to suddenly realize that I was not in control of that vehicle. My car was going gently down an exit ramp with a set of guard rails on both sides. I remember thinking, "Thank goodness for those rails because they would have stopped me if my car had gone too near the edge."

I traveled up the entrance ramp on the other side of the road that crossed the bottom of the exit and continued on my way to school. The strange part is that although there are only four exits between my job and my school, I was never again able to find the exit that saved me; not one of the ones on my path have guard rails on the side. I have driven up and down that section of road trying to find the precise place where I exited and then re-entered the freeway, and none of the entrances or exits look like the one I remember, and none of them have rails.

I'm certain I didn't just dream about or imagine the exit, but I don't know where it is physically located. The feeling that has stayed with me is that I received some kind of special help.

That wasn't the only incident where something unexplainable happened to me. I was traveling behind a pickup truck one time that was loaded with furniture, and received an intense feeling that I needed to move around it. I did so, and almost immediately a large table fell off the back of the truck, landing beside my car instead of directly in front of me causing an accident. At the speed I was going, I would not have been able to stop, and swerving would probably have caused a rollover. Again, I was grateful to the quiet inner voice that offered advice and aid."

*   *   *

Here is another example of "someone else's hand" guiding the wheel of a car in Sandy's story.

Sandy M., 48, Oregon, Parks and Recreation
Sandy's car is guided to a safe lane as a dangerous vehicle rushes past.

"I KNOW THAT I HAVE TWO very special guardian angels who have been with me for a long time, and I think they really helped me out one time where my baby and I would surely have been killed. I was on my way back from the grocery store at dusk. I looked for traffic and it was clear, so I crossed over one lane, went into the left lane and headed for the turn lane.

Suddenly, the wheel of my car spun sharply and I ended up in a safe, non-traffic area outlined by yellow marks. *I knew for a fact that I had NOT rotated that wheel!* In the next second, a car came from out of nowhere and sped past with a "whooshing" sound that meant it must have been going a minimum of 80 mph or more. My car rocked gently from the turbulence, and I uttered a prayer of thanks with a special acknowledgment for my guardian angels. If we had not been suddenly thrust out of the path of danger, the speeding vehicle would have smashed right into the back side door where my four-month old was strapped into a car seat, and Matt would surely have been killed. With the rate of speed they were going, I'm sure I would have died too."

Brent A., 32, Florida, CEO of a frozen food company
A shattering result from boastful antics…

"IN AUGUST OF 1993, I was driving quite late at night with two friends on the almost deserted driveway of the Grand Cypress Resort in Florida after a day of golfing and then some partying. We were in my 4-year old Grand Prix, which anyone will tell you is "my baby." I loved that car! I'll admit I was speeding because I was trying to show my buddies what power, pickup, and "road-holding ability" that car had, which I realize now was probably not the brightest thing to be doing at midnight on a dark road.

The driveway is a curved one, and the car was doing great until we hit a place where the lawn sprinklers had created a wet spot on the pavement right on a curve and the car spun out of control. My beloved Grand Prix skidded straight toward one of the embedded concrete posts that appeared periodically beside the sidewalk bordering the drive.

In a matter of microseconds, the car did another 180 degree turn—it *honestly felt like a giant hand cupped the car* from the top and specifically turned us into this position—and we slammed into the post in the exact center back of the car. The rear end of the car was destroyed, of course, but the amazing thing was that where we hit the post was the one place on that car that guaranteed the least possible injury to the occupants.

We realized afterwards that if we had hit in the front, or broadsided that post on either side, all three of us could have been hurt or killed. By hitting in the back, we were all farthest away from the point of impact, and in fact not one of us had a scratch which was probably better than we deserved.

But the worst consequence was the major damage done to that beautiful car. I don't really know why we were spared from harm, but I have been a more careful driver ever since and have been more attentive to my family—my wife and kids—because everything can be lost in just a second of carelessness.

I can remember another time when I was a kid where the most incredible thing happened in our family when my younger brother was saved from being killed by a terrible fall. I was only four years old and was roughhousing with my brother who was then two years old when the screen popped out of the third floor window and he fell right out. He rolled down the slate roof and disappeared over the edge.

I went in and awakened my parents and told them, "Brian went out the window", which of course created hysteria. My parents raced downstairs and outside, and found Brian lying on a narrow patch of grass that ran alongside the concrete sidewalk. He had sustained absolutely no injuries of any kind and we were astonished that he could land on something not much bigger than he was and miss the sidewalk which would have killed him. We always believed that something, maybe an angel, had been responsible for saving this innocent child."

Gloria F., 55, Northern California, Medical Assistant
Gloria is helped across a frightening crush of traffic despite fears that she would not make it.

"ON PAYDAY ONE TIME, I traveled by bus to the Bank downtown because there was no place for parking anywhere nearby. I was at the intersection of Broadway and MacArthur in Oakland which happens to have an unbelievable *sixteen* lanes of traffic at that point! As I stepped off the curb and began to cross the street, the light had been in my favor, but suddenly it turned yellow. Nervously, I realized that I could not get all the way across the wide street, but thought that I might get to the island that was at the halfway point before the light turned green.

Suddenly a car bumped into me, and I ran alongside for several feet hanging on to the car to keep from falling. My purse flew up into the air, I fell to the street anyway and hit my knee but jumped back up and grabbed my purse, running with a limp toward the other side of the street. By this time, the light had turned green and all the cars from both sides were heading toward me like a wall, and I knew I had to reach the other side or die from being run over!

Almost magically, I was suddenly on the other curb, without really knowing how I had gotten there. *I seemed to have been propelled by some hand that had a power far stronger than my two little feet.* I fell gasping to the curb and just sat there trembling, wondering how on earth I had made it across so many lanes in such a brief couple of seconds. I honestly don't know how this happened and don't believe I had the power myself to get out of this situation. I sat there for several minutes regaining my strength, and thanking the " Spiritual Force" that had magically saved me. I have always felt kind of special ever since."

Sandy J., 50, Arizona, Corporate Trainer, High Tech Industry
Sandy is spared from a snakebite by a swift hand that removes her from danger!

"YEARS AGO, WHEN I WAS PREGNANT with my second child, our family went on a boating picnic to Canyon Lake. The first baby was about a year and a half old and was in a playpen with grandma, so my husband and I took a quiet walk along the shore of the lake.

Suddenly, he stopped dead, gripped tightly the hand that he was holding and said tensely, "Don't say anything…just *run!*" I was so surprised by this that I just dropped his hand and started running straight ahead, not realizing that he had turned and was running the other direction. I wondered why he hadn't passed me—at seven months I was becoming more whale-like each day—and I slowed down in confusion, then stopped dead, horrified as I heard a hissing sound in front of me. I looked down to discover a coiled snake just two feet in front of me and thought I was a "goner."

I realized now that my husband had seen the snake even though I hadn't, and tried to warn me to get away from it. I stood frozen in fear, and uttered a prayer for help. In the blink of an eye, and without moving that I was aware of, I found myself approximately 15 feet away from the snake that was now uncoiling and slithering off into the water. What *angel lifted me up and saved me* I don't know, but in all these years I have never been able to explain how this happened. I am grateful for this blessing because it meant that my child was not endangered."

Kenny K., 35, Arizona, Sanitation Supervisor
A timely "push" keeps a father out of danger.

"IN 1992, MY DAD WAS DOING SOME LOGGING with another man and they were just finishing their loading. They were placing the chains, called a "wrapper", on the load when one of the logs fell off crushing the man my father was working with. Dad said that he literally *felt himself being pushed to safety underneath the truck* and was not hurt at all. He has since felt that this was the most extraordinary thing that has happened in his life."

Sally L., 46, Michigan, Hospital Unit Coordinator
A loving hand reassures a dying young woman.

SALLY SUFFERED THROUGH A VERY DIFFICULT TIME in 1992 with her 18-year-old daughter who became anexoric. The young woman dropped her weight to a skeletal 65 pounds on a 5'7" frame. Although Sally did everything possible to obtain counseling for her daughter, and tried to be extremely supportive and reassuring, the problem escalated as her daughter was unable to respond to those who tried to help. Sally became increasingly alarmed as she began to fear for her beloved daughter's life.

One night, Sally was trying unsuccessfully to encourage her child to eat, and her daughter was lying weakly on a couch. The daughter feebly opened dry lips to whisper in a voice that rustled like dead leaves, "I think I'm going to die now..." With that she closed her eyes and seemed to fade right before Sally's eyes. Panicking, Sally took her pulse, which was a fragile flutter so she decided to get her daughter to the hospital.

"My daughter later told me that she had a very unusual experience in the hospital. She could actually see herself leaving her body and moving toward a tunnel. Suddenly, *my daughter felt strong hands holding her back*, holding her down even, and a voice telling her clearly that she had a purpose in life. She was so strongly affected by this that she knows she experienced a kind of rebirth at that moment. She came back into her body and immediately began to get better.

Today, just one short year later, she is fine and healthy and attempting to create a very positive life for herself. She is also seeking to know the purpose that makes her life a very special and important contribution to the world, one which she doesn't dare take lightly."

Alicia A., 25, Arizona, Banking
An angel eases a difficult birth.

"MY MOTHER SAID I WAS—to phrase this nicely—an unexpected baby and one for which she experienced fairly severe problems. She had gained a tremendous amount of weight, and as an older mother had to take some kind of special medicine to keep from miscarrying. At the time of the birth, she was in terrible pain and said to the doctor, "I'm ready to deliver her." Well, they were still setting up the delivery room, so the doctor said, "Just try to wait a minute." My mother almost shouted back, "If I wait, I'm going to lose this baby!"

The doctor was standing on the other side of the room. Near the doorway, my mother began to see a golden glow that grew in intensity and a shining white figure appeared. My mother told me that the figure had a strong gaze that was incredibly comforting and reassuring and she felt a warmth growing inside her.

I started coming into the world at that moment, and the doctor had to run from across the room to catch me as I slipped out. Boy was he surprised! I was ten pounds and in a breeched position at birth, but there were absolutely no complications and I was born healthy. My mother swore that the presence of an angel helped make that an easy and safe birth, and where she had been frantic and upset before the apparition, she became calm and at peace immediately when she saw the strength emanating from that glowing figure."

Larry T., 52, Arizona, Systems Engineer
A tool magically appears…

"I HAD VOLUNTEERED to do some decorative carpentry at our church and was working with a router on the edges of 4x4 pillars, but had forgotten some things I needed and had to make a trip back home. When I got started again, the router was chewing up the pole and required adjustment, but I did not have the proper wrench with me to do it. Exasperated, I muttered a quick prayer, "Oh Lord, I *really* don't want to have to go back home again…" As I turned around, *there was a wrench lying next to the router*, which I tried and found to be a perfect fit for what I needed. It wasn't my wrench and *hadn't been there before*, and I have no idea where it came from, but I was certainly grateful that it appeared when it did.

The lesson for me in that situation was that the Lord was saying to me, "If I can provide small things, like a wrench, I can provide every other thing you need in your life, for your finances, your career, your relationships, your spiritual growth…everything." This one small incident deepened my faith in a very large way."

DISPATCHING AN ANGEL

Many people believe that angels will help a human by performing a specific task if they are asked. (I suppose we would have to do this nicely...) The process is called "dispatching an angel" and is described very well below by Thelma. The eyes of faith are needed to see this dispatching process at work, and believe that a source of help is readily available to us.

Thelma talks about how an angel helped her in a business setting:

Thelma W., 52, Texas, Author/Speaker
An angel's guidance may influence business ventures...

"AFTER ATTENDING A SEMINAR about angels and how to "dispatch" them, which was a completely new idea to me, I started investigating the work of angels. It was interesting to find that angels have personalities, and that they will direct and guide as well as protect us when asked. I really wanted to test this. I prayed that if an angel wanted to work with me, I would dispatch him or her to a particular Bank where I wanted to do some consulting.

I did this on a Friday, and the following Monday I was on the telephone when my "call waiting" signal alerted me to another incoming call. I picked up that line and it was a woman from the very Bank I had dispatched my angel to. I was elated, almost overwhelmed, and was convinced that "ministering angels" really do work on our behalf when we consciously ask and invite them to assist.

Could this have been just a coincidence, I am asked. While that possibility certainly exists, based on my belief that extraordinary things can happen when angels are involved, I think it was the result of specifically asking for assistance."

LESSONS IN WONDER

1. It is an awesome thought to realize that our lives and destinies can be affected by the gift of help and guidance when we desperately need it.

2. We should not be surprised that seemingly miraculous events occur when we find ourselves in dangerous or threatening situations. We should have a sense of deliberate expectation that "Of course I deserve to have someone on my side who can do extraordinary things!"

3. Our angels appreciate the delight we take in their presence, and our gratitude for the times they extend their hands to aid us.

4. We each should actively ask for the special help we need on a regular basis so that when an alarming situation presents itself, we will receive whatever we need at that moment. Our INTENTION is important, so we must ASK!

5. Angels don't reserve their help for only certain people. EVERYONE can take advantage of this source if they choose to.

PERSONAL JOURNAL

Think about the following, and record any impressions:

1. Have I ever felt a sense of amazement that something unusual or extraordinary had happened to me when I needed help?

2. Was I willing to suspend belief and have a sense of acceptance and wonder that such a remarkable thing would happen to me?

INDIVIDUAL INSIGHTS OR OBSERVATIONS ABOUT "WONDER" IN THE CIRCUMSTANCES OF MY LIFE:

Write in a journal any thoughts that come to mind.

Angels Who Warn of Danger

A Lesson in Listening

LL OF THE PEOPLE YOU WILL MEET in this chapter had an opportunity placed in front of them. They heard internally, sensed, or felt a message that could guide their actions in a way that caused circumstances to change. Most of the people did not have a clear-cut vision of some kind of accident, danger, or problem, but experienced a subtle urging that could not be ignored. Since we do not know future events, listening to this unobtrusive warning from an angel and acting upon it can save us from harm, place us in a position to help someone else, or trigger us to act differently than we otherwise would have. Often, the warning will come in a life-threatening situation, and listening to it will literally save a life.

WARNINGS MAY COME AS A FEELING

Some people experience their warning in the form of a *feeling*, which might be intense or faint. There may not be a logical reason to have this feeling, and often those receiving this subtle message will brush it away. The French word "clairsentience" best describes this feeling, and it is as real as if someone has spoken or touched you. The following stories all demonstrate how heeding a subtle sensation can have a dramatic impact upon someone's life.

Karen S., 51, Michigan, Window Company

A young girl's reluctance to take her usual front-seat position prevents death from a collision with a horse.

"I HAD A GIRLFRIEND who was supposed to go in a large group to a dance. When the van arrived, she became suddenly reluctant to get into the car. She always insisted on sitting in the front seat of a vehicle because she said she needed air, but she just didn't want to get into the front seat of that van. She finally told the others to go on ahead and she would take her own car, and would not budge despite their insistence.

When she arrived at the party, she was surprised to see that the group that had gone before her in the van was not there yet. Surely they would have arrived first since they had left so much earlier... when her friends did not get to party at all she checked to see what had happened, and discovered that there had been a terrible accident.

A horse had trotted into the path of the car and caused a collision severe enough to kill the person in the front passenger seat. If she had gone with the van group as scheduled, she would certainly have been seated in her customary front seat position, right in the path of danger!

When I spoke with my friend afterward, she said that she had received an unusually strong feeling that she should not go in the van. She did not, however, say anything to the rest of the group because she feared that it would sound strange. My friend insisted that she had received a warning that was meant to save her life."

Kristi K., 25, Michigan, Medical Field

For Kristi, the icy chill of the feeling to get away from the lake is as biting as the wind that sweeps its frigid surface.

IN 1985, KRISTI was on a weekend church retreat during February at the Waterloo Recreation Area. She was with a group of about ten people who were out on the frozen lake, "...just goofing around on the ice, something I had done all my life in Michigan. I sure wasn't afraid or anything! Except all of a sudden I did get a tremendously panicked feeling, so overwhelming I almost couldn't move for a minute.

I got icy cold inside and started shivering wildly. The feeling that came over me was that we needed to get off that lake immediately, and I couldn't shake it. It just seemed to get stronger and stronger, and I finally decided I had to do something.

So, I strongly encouraged my group to leave, although they were having such a good time that they really tried to dissuade me from pushing to go. But, thank God, they listened to me and we left the lake area. Good thing! Shortly after that, another group of young people in their 20s who had been on the frozen water at the same time broke through the ice and needed to be rescued by a Coast Guard helicopter.

In fact, one member of that group died and three were injured. I was so thankful that we had been warned because it could have been us. I don't know what encouraged me to go, but it was surely something unusual."

Toni K., 40, Minnesota, Banking

An unusual gust brings with it a terrifying thought: "My son is going to drown!..."

APPROXIMATELY 1985, TONI AND HER FAMILY were enjoying a pleasant summer day by eating outside at their home when an unusual thing happened. Toni describes a "wind" that came up very suddenly and violently that seemed concentrated in their backyard because as she looked at other nearby treetops, they did not seem to be moving with the force that she felt swirling around her patio. As Toni tells it, "Every single hair on my body seemed to stand straight up, and I felt chilled to the center of my being.

I looked at my husband and said, "We've got to get to the river *right now!*", and I turned on my heel and ran for the car in the front yard. As my children told me later, my husband stared at me dumbfounded before they all took off after me. In fact, they barely made it to the car and got in before I was roaring out of the driveway screaming "Oh my God, Aaron is going to drown!"

We raced to the banks of the Mississippi River that was approximately two miles away, and discovered to our horror that our eight-year old son, who was with friends that day, was in the water holding hands with about six other young boys, and they were trying to walk across the river at one of its narrow points. Children just do not understand the power of the currents and the dropoffs that can make even a calm-looking river a deadly trap. And of course, it's in the nature of little boys to be daredevils and try dangerous things when they are in a group.

As an example of what might have been, a week later, a family of four drowned at almost that very spot while they were fishing. One body was pinned deep by currents and wasn't even recovered for more than a week. Something like that could have happened to my son. We were always immeasurably grateful to the Divine help that we received by way of that warning."

Viki T., 44, Michigan, Human Resources

Viki keeps receiving the same weird feeling: "Don't take that boating vacation with the family..."

"MY HUSBAND HAD NOT BEEN IN CONTACT WITH his brothers for 12 years since the family had drifted apart but he did know that some of his relatives lived in

Alaska. We inherited some money that gave us a kind of freedom that we had not known before and we decided as a family that we were looking for an adventurous change.

"Jay" looked up his brothers and reconnected with two of them in Alaska, so we decided to live there for awhile, and simply loved it. We had packed up our two children and were staying with one of the brothers. My husband was offered a job with the City and things were going extraordinarily well.

The families had decided to take a vacation together, but I developed a strong feeling that I really wanted to go back to Michigan for our vacation. All the togetherness was fine, but I just didn't want to go on that planned trip. I wasn't even sure why I was so against it, but the thought of the double family vacation produced really negative feelings.

In the end, I won out and my family came back to Michigan. Imagine our shock later when we learned that a freak storm had blown up on the Alaskan lake where my husband's brother and his children had been vacationing and the eight people in the boat were all killed when it capsized. I have always been thankful for two things...that my husband and his brothers reconnected and appreciated each other before they were separated by death and that my own family was somehow saved."

Leslie K., 23, Oklahoma, Higher Education
Leslie sticks to her original itinerary despite enticements to deviate from it because of a bad feeling about changes.

"IN 1993, I WAS TRAVELING FROM Oklahoma City to Biloxi, Mississippi to visit my boyfriend, and I was on a commuter flight out of Houston into Biloxi. As happens so often today, the airline had overbooked its flight and wanted to bump me, offering me a flight to New Orleans with ground transportation (probably by bus) into Biloxi and in addition, a free roundtrip ticket anywhere in the U.S.

Although the idea of that free ticket was extremely attractive (after all, it would allow me another visit to my friend in the future), as I thought about their offer, I had a really bad feeling in the pit of my stomach. Every time I thought about saying "yes", I got this awful sensation washing over me. For some reason, the idea of going into New Orleans was scaring me to death! I finally went with my gut feeling and refused the offer and went ahead with my commuter flight as planned.

Later that evening, I heard on the news that a bridge had collapsed in New Orleans and several people had been killed. It was a bridge that I would have been traveling over if I had taken the bus or a cab out of New Orleans. When I heard about that, I just knew that somehow I had been warned and had been saved from some kind of danger.

I have since learned to trust what I call my inner voice that lets me know that I am really being protected by someone. The feeling has never left me that I will be alright if I pay attention to that voice."

Gail A., 36, Michigan Health Insurance Company

A fleeting feeling saves some of Gail's precious possessions.

"I KNOW THIS MAY SEEM LIKE A SMALL THING, but I can still remember the time when I was 12 years old and I was getting ready to go to school that I felt a strong feeling I should put some of my possessions into my purse. I picked things that I really had an attachment to like jewelry and such.

At the time, I thought that there wasn't really any reason to do this and was kind of surprised at myself but did it anyway. Imagine how horrified I was when our house burned down before I got back from school that day. Our family lost everything, but at least I had some of my jewelry and pictures and small mementos."

❧

Warnings May Come As Something We Hear

Another way to receive messages is through sound. The practice of "clairaudience" means that someone will hear an actual voice or words giving a warning to avoid danger. What may vary from person to person is whether these voices are heard *inside* one's head or are actually spoken aloud. While we may not always know the exact source of the message, most recipients believe that the giver is a guardian angel or guardian spirit who is watching over a human in desperate need of help.

Cindy S., 47, California, Health Insurance Provider
Cindy's husband is prompted to suggest a detour that removes them from the path of danger.

"I HAD THE MOST INCREDIBLE THING HAPPEN TO ME where I was saved from a certain death one time. I needed to prepare for my mother's funeral, so my husband and I had dropped off our year-old daughter at an aunt's, and were on our way home. We approached an intersection where we *always* turned left; in fact, I don't ever remember a time when we had gone straight through that particular intersection.

Just as we got there, my husband said very abruptly, "Would you like to go over to the A&W?" Now, we never were in the habit of going there and I'm not even that fond of root beer, but for some reason I said, "Sure, that's fine." So, he moved over into the lane that would go straight instead of turning.

Another car pulled up beside us in the lane that was turning left and we both waited briefly at the light. As the light changed, the car that turned left was hit head-on right in front of us in the most horrible accident. This was in the days before seat belts were the law, and bodies were literally flying through the air. I believe that one of the people who was killed by going through a windshield was the passenger in the car turning left, the very place where I would have been sitting if we had gone into that lane instead.

My husband and others rushed to help wherever they could, but I was almost paralyzed with shock to think that we had been only seconds from occupying that lane. I couldn't get it out of my mind that we had never, ever *not* been in that lane except for this one time. To me, this was almost a miraculous occurrence, and for the rest of my life since then, I have always believed that people can be helped in very special and not easily understood ways. This happened about twenty-five years ago, and yet it is as clear and real to me as if it happened yesterday."

Jill L., 26, Minnesota, Sales Manufacturing
An inner voice prevents Jill from being buried under a wall of ice.

JILL RELATED A FASCINATING STORY that shows that angels take special care of children. She certainly had an example of a time when an angel came to her aid when she needed it. "When I was about nine years old, I was walking around my house from the front to the back during the winter. It is important to note that there were sidewalks that ran around both sides of the house, so the back yard was accessible from either direction.

On the side that I had randomly chosen, I was abruptly halted at the front corner of the house by an inner voice that said, "Stop. Do not take this path. Go to the other side of the house." Now, I had always been taught by my mother that I should pay attention to that kind of warning. So I hesitated for a second, and then turned around to go back the way I had come.

As I walked away, the most horrendous crash that I have ever heard took place behind me as a giant wall of ice fell to the sidewalk from the overhang of the roof. This monstrous slab, extending down about ten feet at its longest point, was a melding of icicles that had repeatedly thawed and refrozen layer upon layer for a length of twenty feet along the side of the house.

I stared in absolute horror at a huge pile of debris that had been powerful enough to knock down and bury our metal cyclone fence that bordered the sidewalk on that side of the house. Numb, I realized that but for that tiny alarm I would have been part way down that sidewalk and would have been crushed under hundreds of pounds of ice. I probably would have been killed. After that I didn't have any problem believing that I was being taken care of by someone."

Jill continued, "Our family was always having those kinds of things happening. My four-year-old sister once fell off a third-floor porch that didn't have any guardrails on it and was miraculously saved. Instead of plummeting to the ground, she fell on a double row of clotheslines that broke her fall, bounced her gently, and held her up until someone could rescue her. God must have a special concern for children since so many things could harm them in daily life.

My other sister hurt her back severely in 1992, and had such terrible agony that her doctors scheduled surgery for the slipped disc. The night before the operation, as her children slept soundly upstairs and her husband was away at work, a small "being of light" appeared in her bedroom. She was aware of saying, "So you're here…" before slipping into unconsciousness. When she awoke, my sister was totally pain-free, and the next day her startled doctors (prepared to perform surgery…) could find no physical evidence of any back problem even though her previous x-rays clearly showed the injury."

So who were the miraculous helpers for Jill's sister? Since she has no memory of what occurred, she cannot shed any light upon what may have caused her pain to disappear.

Ann P., 46, Arizona, Administrative Secretary for a City

Kelly's intense message, "Don't go...", prevents her from taking a fatal restaurant excursion.

ANN'S DAUGHTER HAD AN INCREDIBLE EXPERIENCE about 8 years ago when she was 18 years old and a still small voice saved her life. Kelly lived in an apartment with two other girls when a group of friends from their school came by with a van one night to ask them to go to a popular restaurant. "Kelly told me that a little voice inside her kept repeating "Kelly, don't go. Kelly, don't go." It became so insistent that she couldn't ignore it. Her friends thought she was being really strange in saying that she didn't want to go and accused her of being a "wet blanket"; in fact they kept pressuring her strongly.

But she held her ground and refused to leave with the group even though the other girls decided to go. All of her friends were in a terrible accident and were either killed or seriously injured. The van rolled over and one of Kelly's roommates was killed instantly. Although both of the boys and the other girl were badly hurt, they managed to drag their dead friend from the van just a moment before it exploded. In fact, the other girlfriend had severe burns on her leg where pieces of the exploding van landed on her when she couldn't move fast enough to escape them."

Mary R., 45, Michigan, Education

In the dark of night, a car with no lights speeds toward a young woman.

"I HAVE A VERY GOOD FRIEND who was driving on a divided highway after dark with his family in the car. He was startled to hear a clear voice telling him to move out of the lane he was in and into the next lane. Since he thought that was strange and felt he must be imagining this, he ignored the message and didn't react immediately. When he heard the voice a second time speaking with greater urgency, he felt compelled to respond and so he did move over one lane.

Almost immediately, another car driving without headlights on came toward him going in the wrong direction on the highway, and was occupying the lane he had just left. His family was very grateful for that guiding voice."

Connie C., 38, Michigan, Switchboard Operator

The words Connie heard inside her head keep her from walking a dangerous pathway with her small son, a path where a man lurks in the shadow, waiting...

CONNIE RELATED AN EXPERIENCE where she and her young son were specifically warned not to enter a wooded area where they could have been harmed. She lived about five minutes away from her mother with a wooded pathway being the shortest way to go from house to house. A "blind spot" existed in the approximate center of the path where someone had parked a semi trailer, and you could not see a good stretch of the other side of the path from either direction.

As Connie tells it, "I had just left my mother's and was walking home with my six-year-old son. Our normal way would be to take the shortcut on the path. As we came toward it, I saw a man going onto the path from the other direction and a message came into my head, "Be careful, keep your eye on him." Of course, because of that 'ol trailer, he immediately got hid from my view, but I just had a bad feeling that got worse.

Since I couldn't see him anymore, I decided to listen to that strangely persistent voice, and told my son we weren't going to take that path and I wanted him to run to the bowling alley. Of course, he was full of questions. "Why mama?" I said, "You just never mind, and do what your mama says. Now, run!"

As we ran past the entrance to the path on our side, we could see this man crouched down a little ways down that path, just waiting for us. That big 'ol trailer had kept me from seeing him sneak toward us. We were running so fast that he must have decided not to follow because we got to that bowling alley safe.

I know we were saved from danger that night, and I've always believed that if I hadn't listened to that angel voice, my son and I could have been hurt or killed."

Joe W., 43, Arizona, Facilities Manager

Joe is saved by the urgent word "Stop!", seconds before he would have stepped into the path of a speeding pickup truck.

"WHEN I WAS ABOUT EIGHT OR NINE YEARS OLD, I was riding on an old country road in the back of a pickup truck and they stopped to let me off near an intersection. The driver simply stopped in the lane and didn't pull over to the side or anything. As I hopped off, the truck pulled away, and I moved to cross the road toward my driveway.

I couldn't see around the truck that was moving away, but I had barely taken two steps before a voice in my head said, "STOP!" I hesitated in surprise and didn't move for a second, and it was sure a good thing. In the opposite lane, a car was speeding past screened by the pickup truck, and I would surely have been killed if I walked into the other lane."

"I can also remember an incredible thing that happened when I was 16 years old. I was driving my Dad's old farm truck and stopped to pick up a neighbor who wanted to hitch a ride. There were several people already in the cab and in the pickup bed, so our neighbor put one foot in the back of the truck and one on the bumper and just hung on.

Some of the other kids were teasing me to go fast, so I revved it up to about 90 mph for a minute and then skidded to a stop to let my neighbor off. All of a sudden, we had a terrible scare. One of the younger girls in the back had jumped up to grab her hat that the wind had whipped off and she lost her balance and almost went flying off the truck. But because my neighbor was clinging to the side, he caught her and grasped tightly until I slowed to a stop and she was saved.

If he had not been standing in that precise spot, he would not have been in a position to help her and she would have been badly injured or killed as she tumbled to the road. What inspired him to hang on to the back of that truck instead of sitting down is something we can't explain, but it made all the difference in the world."

WARNINGS MAY COME AS A VISION

The French word "clairvoyance", or "clear sight" has most often been used in the context of somehow foretelling the future, but in truth refers to nothing more mysterious than the idea of a mental picture. Many people admit to fleeting visions, images that pass quickly into and out of the mind, although most do not actively seek them, and many often ignore them when they come unbidden.

Those who listen and tune into the mental impressions receive powerful help when they discern what the information means. Sometimes, it means a life will be saved, at other times an accident can be avoided. The stories below are of people who paid attention, and used this extraordinary gift from a guardian to make a difference.

Mare C., 45, Arizona, Arts Commission
A fleeting vision of a car sliding into a ditch prompts a mother to get her children into seatbelts...just in time!

"YOU KNOW, IN THE PAST, I never used to fasten a seatbelt and I'm ashamed to admit that I didn't make my kids use them either. But one time, as we were all driving together, I had a sudden mental flash of our car sliding into a ditch and it seemed rather distinct and very real. I'm so glad I didn't ignore it, but said to my three kids with a really sharp and urgent voice, "Get your seat belts on this second!" They all complied quickly, because that was my "Do it and don't ask any questions!" voice.

I didn't know what the exact danger was, but I was on guard. Within the next couple of minutes, we saw a semi truck which had missed a stop sign skidding towards us with locked brakes on a pretty definite collision course. Just the size of this thing was terrifying and our hearts stopped as the truck slid past with scant inches to spare. Of course, I braked hard when I saw the truck coming, and we slid for what seemed forever, and came to a gentle stop right up against a sign for a canal.

We didn't go into the water or have any damage to the car or the canal sign, and all of the kids were fine, except for being a little scared. I feel it could have certainly turned out differently if I hadn't had the warning for the kids to get secured in the car, and I know that didn't come from my own head."

A strange pattern recurs…
MARE MIGHT BE particularly sensitive to internal non-specific messages, because she told me several other things that don't quite fit an easy explanation. When she was working for another city department in 1991, the numbers 1,2,3, and 4 kept popping unbidden into her head. She would constantly see a visual stimulus for those numbers: for example, she would look at a clock and it would read 12:34, she would glance at a house number and it would be 1234 xyz street, or she would be given a store receipt and it would be for $12.34 or issued at 12:34 p.m.

This odd random occurrence went on for *several months* until she was suddenly bumped from her existing job to a new department. Imagine Mare's surprise when she was informed that the security code for her new building included the numbers 1,2,3, and 4. After that, the strange coincidences stopped.

A mother's comfort…just when needed.
MARE HAD ANOTHER UNUSUAL kind of visitation regarding her mother who had died when Mare was 19. In 1990, (26 years after her mother's death) her mother

came to her in a dream shortly after Thanksgiving. It was a very comforting dream...Mare's mother got up from where they were sitting at a small, round table, came around and hugged her saying, "I love you, everything will be alright."

A few days later, Mare's brother had an unexpected, severe heart attack at the age of 43, followed by two additional attacks while she was driving to the hospital where he was (about 45 miles away). Although she feared she might lose him too, the doctors were able to save his life with angioplasty. Her mother was correct, everything did turn out alright, and Mare carried with her the soothing memory of a long-gone parent still watching over the needs of her children.

Lynnette M., 39, California, Orthodontics
A vision of red, accompanied by crashing noises, haunts a young woman until the day that she is the only one who can prevent a horrible collision.

"WHEN I WAS A TEENAGER, a very odd kind of feeling that was accompanied by sound effects happened continuously for several weeks. I would hear a crashing sound that seemed very loud except that it would happen inside my head and no one else could hear it. In fact, when it happened, I would think, "I must have imagined this; there's nothing around me."

Usually, this would occur only during the day, and on a totally random basis. Often, I became apprehensive and nervous when it happened. Immediately after the sound, I would "see" something that could either be a red wave that washed toward me but didn't touch me, or it could be like a glass window that I was standing in front of and someone would throw red paint which splashed all over it. My heart would begin palpitating and I was very frightened when this happened, but after a short time, it would go away and the feelings of fright would diminish so I would forget about it.

One day, a friend called and asked me to go with her to another friend's house which was about a half hour away. I immediately had a bad feeling about this and at first refused, but she pressed me to go with her so I gave in. I felt anxious the entire trip and had a feeling of terror that I just couldn't shake.

On the way back, we arrived at a four-way stop sign and stayed there for a moment. The feelings that had been building for weeks seemed to come to some kind of final, oppressive climax and I felt as if I was suffocating for a second. My friend started into the intersection when it was her turn, and I suddenly screamed, "Margaret, don't go. Wait!" She was so surprised that she just stopped dead, and at that very moment, a truck raced through the stop sign and the intersection, and I realized with horror that we would have been directly in its path if we had continued.

The truck would have most certainly struck us with terrible consequences. As the truck passed, and we continued in a somewhat dazed way, I realized that my feelings of terror had subsided, and very quickly disappeared. It was most strange, but I realized over the next few days that my "crashing sound", and vision of red washing over me was gone, never to return.

The only conclusion that I can draw from this is that there had been the potential for a horrendous accident in which my friend and I could have been injured or killed. Somehow, the warning that I felt compelled to give had changed those circumstances, and we had been somehow saved from a terrible fate. I always felt that the sounds and visions that had been coming to me for several weeks before this incident were a warning even though I did not truly understand the nature of the information. Someone was certainly taking care of me!"

Christine C., 47, Indiana, Realty Office
A "slow motion movie" allows Christine to "see" a young child dash out in front of her moving vehicle.

"I HAD NEW BRAKES PUT on my car in 1990 and noticed that the wheel area started smoking while I was taking my kids to school. Since I had a meeting at Church that night, I decided to take our truck to it so I wouldn't have any problem with the new brakes in case they weren't working right. Our town is fairly small and has a 4-way stop sign in the center, which I had to stop at. As I was doing that, I saw a group of about a half-dozen children farther down the block. While I watched, a couple of the older boys darted across the street away from the group.

The only way to describe what happened next was that it was like frames of a movie that you watch in slow motion. I saw my truck moving slowly like a series of blurred images one frame at a time out in front of me and in that vision, as I approached the group one of the little kids, about a two-year old, ran out after the older boys directly in front of my truck.

Because I had seen this happening in the "slow motion" vision, I already had started to brake as I came toward the group, so that I was going very slowly when I actually arrived near them. Just as I had envisioned in my "movie", one of the smallest children ran out in front of me, but I was going slowly enough that I was able to brake with no problem and I did not hit the child. If I had not seen the "slow motion, blurred images", I would not have slowed down and I know that I would have struck that little one because I did not have enough time to stop safely."

* * *

The warnings cannot always be easily broken down into feelings, words, or mental pictures. Sometimes people just act in a way that surprises them or is unexpected, but is ultimately for the best.

The remaining stories in this chapter are of precipitous actions, where someone was prompted to simply "do" something, an instantaneous response that helped at the moment and made a difference for the person involved.

Chanita H., 24, Michigan, Hospital Secretary

When Chanita abruptly moves from one lane to another, her life is saved from a charging deer.

IN 1990, CHANITA HAD PLANNED a trip to see a sister who was at college in Nashville, Tennessee. About three days before the trip she became extremely anxious about her car, but wasn't sure what this feeling meant. She didn't feel like going out or using her car and wouldn't allow anyone else to use it either. She felt that her car was somehow in danger.

As the day of her trip approached, she determined to go anyway because she didn't want to disappoint her sister and she had looked forward to the trip also. She had a friend check out the car, and he determined that absolutely nothing was wrong.

Everything seemed fine as Chanita traveled through Michigan, Indiana, and on into Kentucky, and she began to relax. She was driving at night on a Kentucky freeway when she was engulfed with a fear of an impending accident. This sensation was almost suffocating her when she saw a sign that said "Deer Crossing" and made a sudden decision to just get off the highway and calm down for a few minutes.

She had seen a rest area sign about a half mile back and knew that one was going to be coming up shortly. Chanita tells the rest: "I jerked the wheel of that car, and pulled out of the fast lane, into the center, and then into the slow lane because I knew the exit for the rest area would be there awfully quick and didn't want to miss it.

As I crossed the lanes and slowed down, the car that had been traveling behind me—those lights had been in my mirror for the last twenty miles— overtook me and came alongside, then slowly pulled ahead, still in the far left, fast lane.

Suddenly there was a terrible crashing noise, and that car went out of control.

I was so shocked I could hardly think! I did stop, though, to see if I could do anything to help, and couldn't believe what an awful mess! A huge deer had jumped with no warning from the woods right into the car, had totally destroyed the whole side of the car, and was in that man's back seat. He had not had any time at all to react or help himself.

The man was hurt, but seemed able to stay with the car while I went to the rest area to find a phone to call for help. I'm amazed my fingers worked on the phone buttons I was so shook up; I know my voice was shaking when I talked to the operator.

I don't think I'm real religious or anything, although I've always thought that people have a kind of "sixth sense" about things. But maybe I'm ready to believe that there's more to it than that after what happened to me. I was real lucky, but maybe it was more than that."

Barb S., Washington State, Software Development Company
By changing lanes, Barb and her husband remain safe.

"MY HUSBAND AND I WERE RETURNING from motorcycle races one night, and it was very late, probably around 3 a.m. We were traveling in the fast lane of the freeway and my husband was getting tired, so I told him that I would drive and he could go into the back and go to sleep.

He said he would like to do that but wanted me to pull immediately out of the fast lane and asked it with quite a bit of urgency. I thought it was an odd request because there was only one car ahead of me and nobody behind me so it was almost like driving on a deserted road. However, I did as he asked.

A few seconds after I switched into the next lane, out of nowhere came a car going at least 100 miles per hour in the fast lane that I had just vacated and slammed into the rear end of the vehicle that had been ahead of me in that lane.

If I had not moved over when I did, it would have slammed into us and we would probably have been killed because my husband's motorcycle and the gasoline for it was in the back and would have exploded on impact!"

Hope G., 28, California, Manufacturing
A warning rock prevents Hope from falling asleep at the wheel of her speeding car.

"MY EX-HUSBAND LIVES ABOUT six hours away from me in Sacramento, and I had driven my son there for a visit one time when we had a very frightening experience on the way home. The visit had been rushed, and because of all the driving, I had not really had very much sleep. I was returning to southern California and was struggling to stay awake, playing the radio very loudly and riding with the window down to blow some air through the car. It was about noon, and I was driving on Highway 99 toward I-5, when I literally drifted off to sleep behind the wheel of the car.

Suddenly, I was jolted awake by a rock approximately the size of a fist that hit the windshield with a terrible crash, but surprisingly did not crack or shatter the glass. That is very unusual considering that often a tiny pebble can cause a crack. I was the only car on the road at that point, and there was nothing nearby that the rock could have fallen from. It was almost as if someone had just pitched this thing into the very middle of my windshield.

This incident startled me so much that I had adrenaline shooting through my system and instantly felt very wide awake. In fact, I had no problem staying awake for the next several hours of my trip. I was so scared that I could have killed both my son and myself that I truly believe that someone, like an angel, was trying to help me and wake me up. There doesn't seem to be any other explanation because no one else was on the road with me at that point. I was always grateful for receiving that special wake-up call before it was too late."

*   *   *

Each of the stories recorded in this section is remarkable in the reality that something could have turned out quite differently for the person. Death was lurking, danger in a vehicle was imminent, serious illness was present, or some other catastrophe loomed; and the threat was avoided by attention to a small voice, vision, or feeling inside. We are often so bombarded by environmental noise that we are losing our ability to hear internal promptings. Our goal is to learn how to tune in to a different channel that offers us a tremendous gift—the help of an angelic voice that comes to our aid.

LESSONS IN LISTENING

1. A warning doesn't always make a lot of noise inside our head. The words can be as soft as a wisp of breeze. Or it can be a feeling so slight that we could push it away in a second.

2. We must listen the first time, and not begin a conversation inside ourselves where we debate endlessly whether or not the warning makes sense logically. Those few seconds can mean life or death. We must learn to listen instantly and then respond.

3. We may sometimes have misgivings about what we are hearing, or it may be a message that we wish we weren't receiving because we don't like the news. However, once we learn to trust better, we will be more open to listening for warnings or communication regardless of our feelings about it. These messages are always meant for our good.

4. Our ability to learn to listen for warnings will have an impact on the people around us because many times those warnings are meant to help them too.

PERSONAL JOURNAL

Think about the following, and record any impressions:

1. In what circumstances did I ever have a feeling that I needed to avoid something, get out of a situation, or react immediately?

2. What happened right after that?

3. Did the results show that circumstances could have been very different?

4. What did I notice about the message…did I hear words inside, was it a "gut feeling", did I just find myself "spontaneously" doing something that surprised me?

5. What will I "LISTEN FOR" in the future?

INDIVIDUAL INSIGHTS OR OBSERVATIONS
ABOUT "LISTENING" IN MY LIFE:

Write in a journal any thoughts that come to mind.

CHAPTER FIVE

Angels Who Protect Us

A Lesson in Serenity

THE STORIES IN THIS CHAPTER all involve help received in a moment of danger or a perilous situation where the person in need of assistance has no other option, and no other resource to turn to. The aid being given often brings a sudden calm and serenity to an emotionally-charged situation.

In some cases, the help is sought through a hurried prayer or wordless plea; in others, it is an unexpected and serendipitous gift. Sometimes the certainty that "someone else is taking care of me…" is enough to trigger a sense of peace. At that point people let go of fear, anxiety, and frustration; and surrender to the certainty that they are not alone. It is enough for them.

The lesson for today's world, in which anxiety and fear are the norm, is that we too have the potential for assistance from our protectors, the angels, when our circumstances are menacing. Asking and then receiving whatever we need will bring the peace we cherish.

Jeralee B., 51, Oregon, Pianist and Piano Teacher

A missionary family faces fear and death...and triumphs! An unusual teacher provides the secret of the rooster...

JERALEE GREW UP on the wonderful stories shared by her relatives about their experiences as evangelists. She always took for granted that these are not unusual or extraordinary events, but very much to be expected by those who believe in God's power. The stories below are her favorites, and are typical of the almost miraculous things that can happen when one simply trusts that God will prevail.

"My uncle and aunt, Carroll and Doris Tamplin, acted as missionaries for the World Gospel Missions in South America during the '40s and '50s. While they were in Bolivia, they were trying to approach a tribe of particularly unfriendly Indians who, in fact, had been known to have murdered several outsiders. One time, before they were leaving to initiate an encounter with the Indians, the Prayer Team prayed specifically for direction to guide them about what to do.

While they were praying, a person appeared who was dressed in native garb and spoke to them, "Go into the village and find the street with this name (he gave exact directions about where to turn to find the location), locate this house, go behind the house and you will find a red rooster. Take this rooster, and the person who leads the party must hold it high where it can be seen, and you will be safe." After imparting this information, the stranger disappeared.

The team did as they were directed and found the rooster exactly as their helper had stated, so they took it on their expedition. When they arrived in the jungle, before long their path was blocked by a large group of extremely aggressive Indians with wildly painted faces and bodies, who brandished menacing-looking spears. As the natives shouted in an unfamiliar language, the leader remembered the admonition of the stranger and took the red rooster holding it high over his head, shaking it at the group. Suddenly, the Indians stood transfixed and stopped screaming and chanting, instead standing quietly with their spears down on the ground.

Someone with the Tamplins' party spoke a dialect fairly close to the natives', and although they did not speak the identical language, the evangelizing team slowly discovered an amazing thing. The leader of the native group had had a dream in which he had seen a person holding a red rooster and had been told in his dream that whoever brought this was a friendly people who should be listened to with respect. Before this, because no one spoke the natives' language, there was no way to communicate with them to inform the natives that the visitors were friendly and meant no harm. Out of fear and ignorance, the natives had previously killed the strangers they feared brought them danger.

Because they had an opening to sit down and meet the Indians in a non-threatening way, the missionary group was very successful at approaching and then working with the natives."

* * *

A desperate prayer summons huge guards to endangered missionaries.

"ON ANOTHER OCCASION, the missionary team was traveling from village to village on one of its expeditions and did not know where to sleep when it became quite late. The group decided to just put their mats down along the side of the road and rest for awhile. Before long, a friendly native came by and told them that this was not at all safe, and took them to a hut where they were to spend the night.

The grateful group had knelt down to say their night prayers when they began to hear a commotion outside the hut. There was angry shouting, chanting, and the flickering glare of burning torches throwing long, dark shadows on the flimsy walls of their shelter. Afraid to go outside to find out what this meant, the group huddled in the center terrified, fearing that they would be murdered at any moment. Suddenly, one member of the party said boldly, "What are we cowering here for? We're doing God's work! Don't we believe that He will take care of us? Our faith is certainly weak if we doubt His assurances!"

Everyone realized that of course this was true, and so together they knelt down and prayed, "Lord, we are here doing the work you have led us to do. We ask you now to place your angels around us and protect us here in this dwelling." This prayer gave the group members tremendous comfort, and they simply were no longer frightened. They just put down their pallets and went peacefully to sleep as the noise thundered on around them.

The next thing they knew, it was a beautiful and quiet morning outside and as they ventured out, they found nearby some of the friendly natives that they had been working with. Curious, the team inquired about the screaming and shouting they had heard the night before. Excitedly, the friendly natives told them that a really bad tribe of Indians had learned they were there inside and had come and wanted to kill them. However, they had finally been frightened away by the *very large men* who had been outside guarding the hut.

The team members smiled at one another as they thought about the prayer they had said, knowing that it must have been the Angels of God protectively standing guard outside. It was a good lesson about not doubting the Lord's promises."

Margaret S., Arizona, Retired

A potential assailant "sees" something so fearsome that he runs away.

YEARS AGO, MARGARET WAS TAKING night classes at a Junior College in Tulsa, Oklahoma and often parked a good distance from campus to save money on her parking fees. One night a professor kept the class longer than normal and she was walking through darkened streets to get to her car. Margaret was crossing a deserted intersection when a man drove up spewing obscenities, but she ignored him and walked on because she had taken a safety training class that suggested not engaging in any kind of verbal or nonverbal contact. When the car blocked her path, she walked purposefully around it, a firm and confident stride belying the rapidly racing heart and twisting stomach.

Initially, Margaret was angry with this person and then prayed for him because he clearly had some kind of emotional or mental problem. She continued for another couple of blocks and was almost to her vehicle when she saw his car pull up in front of her again, and he got out, walking toward her! Another car was coming behind him down the one-way street, and Margaret waved her arm frantically trying to flag it down, but it wouldn't stop! At this point she was becoming very frightened.

That very afternoon, her boss had given her a thank you card for a Christmas gift with a quote from Is. 41:10 about "Fear not, I am with you…I will strengthen you and help you, and uphold you with My right hand of justice." Those words leapt to her mind and she began saying them aloud. The words were at first trembling and soft, then stronger and louder. "All of a sudden, a sense of utter peace came over me and my fear just vanished. Intellectually, I knew I was in a very dangerous situation, but emotionally I was feeling calm. It was the most incredible thing!

I faced my potential assailant directly and stood my ground, with the words of Isaiah ringing out in that street in a clear, confident tone. When the man got very close to me, he stopped suddenly and stared over my shoulder with a look of *absolute horror* and his mouth dropped open… What was he seeing? Instantly, he turned and ran back to his car just as fast as he could, got in, and took off with a tremendous squealing of tires.

I continued on the short distance to my own car and arrived safely home. To this day, I have often wondered what he saw…some member of the heavenly host sent as promised by God to act as my fierce guardian?"

Unusual help at a marathon…

WHEN MARGARET WAS WORKING at Oral Roberts University, she and her husband who were both fitness buffs had pre-registered for a marathon. Margaret later realized that she had also accidentally scheduled a physical fitness test through the University's health program for the day before the marathon. She wavered…should she cancel the appointment for the test? The problem was that they were very hard to get, and rescheduling could be a major headache. So Margaret decided to try to do both.

"During the fitness test, they ran me to exhaustion on a treadmill, and the next day I found myself feeling very tired right from the beginning of an extremely hilly race. I began to think I should just quit running, but instead prayed for an angel to give me strength. Shortly after that, I noticed a runner come up behind me and then stay abreast of me for awhile. He called me by name so I figured it was someone from the University, probably the man who was sometimes running around the track when I was there too. In fact, I decided that's who it was because there was a distinct resemblance. He ran beside me for quite some time, and offered encouragements such as "Lean into the hill this way, c'mon you can do it" and then later just ran on in front.

I could see him in the distance and one time he turned around and was running backwards, waving at me. Soon he was gone from sight. Later, when my husband and I were running together, I became so physically spent that I knew I couldn't finish and told him that I planned to drop out. Suddenly, my friend was back with us, calling both my husband and me by name and encouraging both of us to continue. It didn't occur to me at the time that I had not passed him on my course so how could he be behind us? My husband said, "Do you know that guy? Who is he?" I replied, "I think he's from school because I see a guy on the track sometimes who runs backwards like that. It must be him."

We finished the race, and did it with an exceptionally good time—and in fact we were surprised at just how well we did. The only weird thing…I saw my fellow staff member later and realized he didn't really look like the man from the race after all, but I asked him anyway, "Did you run the marathon?" He replied, "No, I never run those." I then decided that an angel had come to encourage us because I remembered a movie I had seen with my husband which was about runners and had an angel theme. In that film, an angel had run backwards. I realized that my angel might have expected me to recognize him when he was running backwards waving at me."

Margaret's husband also had an odd experience when he was alone doing a triathlon. He had fallen during a night race and had broken his flashlight, so he couldn't see the white flour markings used to mark the trail. The flashlight would shine on the flour and show the runner the way. He got off the trail somehow and became very worried, because the issue now was not about missing the rest of the race but about being lost in the dark. He prayed for help, and suddenly a light was shining down on the trail some distance away and as he ran toward it he saw the flour and got back on the trail. Her husband did very well in that race, placing third in his age group.

Kim A., 22, Oregon, Insurance Industry
Again, missionaries are protected when threatened.

"AFTER I GRADUATED FROM HIGH SCHOOL, I was with friends on a mission trip to Miami, Florida. We were in "Little Havana" and I was part of a group of adults and teenagers who were walking to our apartment when we were accosted by a gang. The gang members had driven by us, stopped, and got out of their car, approaching us in a very threatening manner.

We just began singing hymns of praise and would not act afraid. When the gang got close to us, they suddenly had the most terrified looks on their faces, turned around and ran to their car and raced away. We were left standing there alone, slightly shaken but extremely thankful."

Diana G., 42, Texas, Employment and Training Agency
Diana's house is protected in a most dramatic and strange way.

WHEN A RELATIVE PASSED AWAY IN 1992, Diana's husband Ralph had driven four hours to attend the funeral, but discovered enroute that his own mother had become seriously ill following an angioplasty. Upon learning the news, Ralph had an opportunity to spend a short time with his mother and tell her goodbye. Sadly, she died shortly after that. Ralph immediately turned around to return and pick up his family for his mother's funeral. Diana was waiting for him and had started to cook some chicken since he had not had time to eat. Ralph was anxious to get on the road however, and didn't want to eat, so they packed the car and left immediately, arriving at his sister's house around 3 a.m.

Diana was exhausted and desperately wanted to fall asleep, but was startled to hear the voice of her just-deceased mother-in-law calling, "Diana, you left the stove on, darling." Even more astonishing was the wispy white vision of her husband's mother on top of the dresser. Diana realized in shock that she really was seeing something and that it was true—she didn't remember turning the chicken off. She prayed " Dear God, please protect our home." Turning to the floating figure, she entreated, "Mom can you help me here, can you take care of the house for us?"

Distressed, Diana called the friends who were watching the house and asked them to check in the morning and turn off her stove. Oddly, she didn't feel a sense of urgency that anything terrible would happen, so she didn't ask them to go over immediately. At 6 a.m., she received a call that her friends had checked her kitchen and the burner was, in fact, *turned on;* but the *element was stone cold.* The chicken had cooked for hours, but there was no heat and it was not burned.

Diana asked her friend over the phone to leave everything as it was, and when she returned home, she checked the burner carefully. When she turned it on, the element immediately began to heat and heated to full strength. To this day, Diana believes that Ralph's mother saved their home.

Sherry W., 32, Texas, Homemaker
A young boy is protected as he slips beneath the wheels of his mother's car.

"MY FRIEND RHONDA has a seven-year-old son Cody who plays in the same Little League my child does, and I was very concerned one time when they didn't show up for a banquet. I checked on them later and discovered that a crisis had occurred when Rhonda returned in the rain from a shopping trip.

As she turned into the dark, wet, dirt driveway, Rhonda heard a loud crunching, scraping sound like metal being caught beneath the car. Startled, she slammed on the brakes and stopped immediately, thinking that she had run over a child's bicycle left out accidentally in the rain. She got out of her Dodge Caravan to check, primarily so that she wouldn't damage her car which was her main concern at that point. Instead, to her horror, she found her son Cody trapped under the front wheels of the van which is the heaviest part since that's where the engine is. He had run out to greet her and slipped in the mud, falling underneath the vehicle.

Rhonda rushed Cody to the hospital, and he told her along the way about the two men who had talked to him. He saw them as extremely large men who warned him to be very still and not move or struggle and assured him that he would be fine. Cody had tried to obey them and not move. At the hospital, he checked out O.K. except for a bruised kidney which was a minor injury considering what he could have suffered.

Rhonda is convinced that the angels who helped Cody caused her to hear a non-existent sound to force her to stop since there was nothing crunchy or metal involved. The quick braking had prevented the rear wheels from hitting him too which might have caused far more serious injury. They both believe strongly that Cody had an encounter with angels."

Sherry's friend Ron sells a condo...
SHERRY ALSO HAS A FRIEND Ron who had an unusual incident which defies explanation occur to him. Ron was trying to sell his condo and had an unexpected opportunity to move, but was in a quandary about signing the lease for fear that the condo wouldn't sell. He didn't want the burden of two payments for a long period of time. He needed to decide this over a weekend, so he prayed for guidance: Should he commit to this lease or not? Shortly afterward, he received a phone call from a man who said he saw an ad in the Arizona Republic and wanted to come to the condo to check it out.

Ron was puzzled because he hadn't placed an ad in that paper, in fact, he checked to see it and couldn't find anything. The only ad he had running at that time was in the Pennysaver. A young man and woman came to look, walked quickly through (Ron feels they didn't do the normal things they would like open closets etc.), said they were definitely interested but would give first names only. He questioned them again about the ad, but they insisted it had been in the Republic newspaper.

Later he thought maybe they had been mistaken about the name of the newspaper and really meant the Tribune so he checked *all the papers,* and still found nothing. Ron decided that this encounter was, instead of a possible sale, simply a sign that he should trust and commit to his lease, which he did. He never saw the young couple again, but his condo did sell shortly after that.

Paul R., 42, Arizona, Government Utility
A van loaded with young students misses a turnoff and heads straight for a Ponderosa pine...

"ABOUT 1988, I WAS TRAVELING in the San Bernadino Mountains by Lake Arrowhead in California with a group of junior-high aged kids on a church retreat. We were headed for an ice-skating party, and I had about 12 or 13 kids sitting on the floor of a Volkswagen van. At a place called the "Blue Jay turnoff", I missed the corner, and although I was not speeding I careened off the road. We were headed straight toward a Ponderosa pine tree, and it was only a few feet away—I didn't even have time to yell at the kids or hit the brake...I just closed my eyes and expected an impact.

I felt a sharp jerk and a swaying sensation, and when I opened my eyes a second later, we were back traveling straight down the road. The kids thought this was great—they were rolling from side-to-side and shouting in the back and hollered something about "cool driving..."

It was my twisting stomach and rapidly-beating heart that told me that something very unusual had happened. What was it? I had expected a windshield to explode on me any second, and my kids to be injured, but by some miracle we were all safe. The only thing I can believe is that there was some kind of angelic intervention."

Sandra W., 55, Missouri, Consultant/Author
A frightened domestic violence victim receives extraordinary help as she is thrown over a balcony.

"I WAS IN THE MIDDLE OF A DIVORCE, and preparing to move myself and my three children out of the house that my ex-husband still occupied. Although the paperwork had already been processed and at this point we were officially divorced, I was still at our home. One of my friends from school, a man, called to check on me one day, and although we had the most general of conversations…along the lines of "Hope you're doing O.K." and "Thanks for your interest, I'm fine", I still felt a little apprehensive when I heard an extension phone hang up as I put my own phone receiver down. My ex-husband charged into the room and said, "Who were you just talking to?" I answered somewhat coolly, "Since we are no longer married, I don't think that is really any of your business." With that, he exploded and lunged toward me, chasing me around the house into the area of the master bedroom.

I started screaming loudly, which surprised me a little because I had never done that before. Toward the end of our marriage, he had beaten me two different times, and I had been silent, not crying out or making any sound. It may seem foolish now, but I didn't want anyone, either our children or on one occasion our houseguests, to know that this was happening. My feelings were ones of embarrassment and shame so I hid the brutality, not realizing that this played right into my husband's needs for control and dominance.

As I screamed and dodged left and right around furniture, we ended up near the balcony of the bedroom. The noise had brought out our neighbors who yelled up at me, "Do you want us to call the police?" My answer must have seemed very strange… "I don't know." At this point, I heard a voice in my head say with absolute conviction, certainty, and authority, "No matter what happens, at all times remain calm." This statement was repeated three different times, and I found myself going limp as I heard it.

This distracted me for a moment and I lost my concentration on escape, which allowed my husband to grab me with a final burst of strength. He picked me up and threw me over the railing of the balcony which had approximately a fifteen-foot drop to the ground. The neighbors were standing there watching, and someone screamed.

It was later that an observer said to me, "It was the most unbelievable thing…you just hung suspended in the air for a moment, then your body floated back toward the house, and fell inside the railing onto the balcony." I know that the side of my face was scraped by the railing, so it was a very close thing.

As I think about it now, I don't remember being aware of the passage of time at all. My neighbors called the police at that point, so I did receive help after that. While I have always had a strong faith, after this incident, I knew that I was being protected in a very special way, and it has influenced my life in more ways than I can express."

Ed K., 57, Arizona, Field Technician
A teenager could have accidentally crushed the stranded baby stroller beneath the wheels of his car.

"IN 1956, I HAD JUST RECEIVED my first driver's license and like all 16-year-olds was dying to have opportunities to use it! About three months after I started driving, I was in my beloved 1949 Dodge on a beautiful breezy fall day in New Jersey. In front of a downtown deli, I stopped, angled my car perfectly, and got ready to slide into a parallel parking space. I was a really good parallel parker.

My left hand gripped the steering wheel as usual, my right arm was spread across the back of the seat, and my body was twisted looking over my right shoulder... perfect position! Except I couldn't move the car... I was absolutely immobilized for several minutes, as if I had been frozen in time. It was almost like I didn't know what to do next, or had forgotten how to complete this move.

All of a sudden as I waited, a woman raced over from the opposite side of the street, picked up a baby in a stroller which had rolled down a slight incline of the sidewalk and had tipped over into the gutter behind the right rear tire of my car.

Apparently the mother had gone into the deli for just a moment leaving the stroller by the door, and the woman on the opposite side had seen the stroller fall into the street. This was an absolute blind spot for me; I could never have known that the child was there.

There were a couple of odd things that were part of this. All of my windows were down and yet I remember total silence, no woman's voice screaming at me to "Stop!". I had been gripping the steering wheel so hard that my hand was sweaty, and the muscles in the other arm over the back seat were very stiff. I don't know exactly how long I couldn't budge, but after the baby was safely back on the sidewalk, it was as if time began to move again and I suddenly and smoothly completed my parking maneuver.

It's as if I was being held in place by a giant hand until the child's life could be saved. I've really never told anyone about this for 37 years except maybe two priests because I thought perhaps they could understand what happened on that street. Anybody else would think I was just plain crazy. I know for certain that all those years ago I wasn't sure how religion, faith, and God fit into people's lives, but I am 100% sure now that God is present, active, and cares about what happens to the smallest of us. That one experience changed my life."

Dorothy L., 32, Minnesota, Dental Office
A father's life is at stake when he is trapped between the spikes of a rock crusher.

DOROTHY'S FATHER BEN was performing maintenance at a sewer plant in Red Wing, Minnesota in 1972. He was cleaning out the conveyor of a rock crusher which took half-ton chunks of rock and clay and reduced them to a gravelly substance. The roller pins of this machine were approximately 8-10 feet high with about 12-inch spikes. Ben asked a coworker to turn on the conveyor belt, but this was a new employee who misunderstood and instead turned on the crusher, then accidentally fell across the lever that he could have used to stop the machine.

"As Dad started to go between the rollers, and at the point where a spike had already penetrated both of his legs, inexplicably a shear pin broke that jammed the machine and halted its 400 horsepower motor. *This was a most unusual occurrence since the shear pins were checked constantly as part of routine maintenance, and there was no excuse for this one to break!* This was a critical thing because the other employee would have been unable to stop the machine so quickly since the lever was trapped beneath him when he tripped. Dad was stuck firmly where the spikes had caught his legs just below the knees, and they had to take the rollers apart to get him out. It was cold (10 degrees below zero) and he was numb, but he kept his faith that everything would turn out alright, praying aloud and even joking with his rescuers."

Ben later personally verified that he was in that crusher for five and a half hours, and it took 3 acetylene torches to cut out the 9" drive shaft to release him. This was a precarious task because if they slipped even slightly, they would reverse the rollers which would then crush him in the other direction. The freezing cold iron actually was a benefit for Ben because it limited the bleeding where his legs had been penetrated by the spikes.

"When they finally got Dad cut out of the machine and to the hospital, the doctor said it was the worst accident of this type he had ever seen. Dad was in the hospital for over three months, and when released, he had casts up to his thighs and could only get around in a wheelchair. He was in rehabilitation for months, and walked first with crutches and then with a cane. Unfortunately, gangrene set in on one side and he lost four toes on one of his feet. When the accident happened, there were ten kids in our family aged 9-22, so it was hard for the family to have this tragedy occur. We always felt that Dad had been taken care of in a very special way to have lived through the incident and its aftermath."

Terri S., 33, Arizona, Civil Engineering

A bullet out of the dark threatens an innocent driver—did the static on the radio send a message?

TERRI IS THE WOMAN WHO was comforted by the mysterious "encyclopedia salesman" who came to her door. She had another extremely unusual experience in which she believes she was saved from being killed by a bullet fired by an unknown assailant.

"In 1993, I was out about 12:30 a.m. with a friend hanging up signs for a garage sale that we were planning to hold the next day. I would drive to a designated place, stop, and he would jump out and hang up the sign. At one place I pulled into a bus bay, and he ran out to hang a sign on a pole at the corner. As I sat there a moment, I heard a sudden, loud burst of static on my radio which was very strange because it had not done that before.

I leaned over to adjust the dial thinking how odd it was to have that occur when a bullet came through the window on my side of the car, whizzed directly past the back of my head, and went out the other side where the door was standing open. Someone had shot at me! I was so shocked I could barely believe it. We waited there and called the police but didn't have much information to go on. It seemed to be a random drive-by attack by someone who did not know us.

The really weird thing that happened was that the officer had me sit in the normal position in the driver's seat so that he could judge the angle of the bullet, and if I had not bent over exactly at the moment I did, the bullet would have struck me directly in front of my ear. I would have been killed instantly, the officer said.

It is very sobering to have something like that happen because you realize just how vulnerable and helpless you really are against random violence. It let me know in a very powerful way that someone was looking out for me and I truly do believe that I had an angel at my side. I cannot believe that the static on my radio was a chance event that just happened at that moment by accident."

Allan S., 56, Arizona, Civil Engineer

A young survey worker falls upon a chain saw that promises certain mutilation or death.

WHEN ALLAN WAS WORKING for the Forest Service on a survey crew one summer during college, he was assigned the job of clearing away brush from a particular area. He and his fellow crew members were running a chain saw at full speed when he slipped on weeds or grass as he held some brush over for the person cutting.

Allan fell with his head directly on top of the running chain saw and a miraculous thing happened. "The saw suddenly stopped one second before I hit my head on the blade. This was very odd because it was the only time that day the saw had died: it worked dependably right up until that moment, and it never stopped again until we quit work for the day.

I truly have no explanation for how the saw could stop at that exact second in order to save my life. At the time, I thought it was an incredibly lucky accident that the engine died, but over the years I have come to believe that it was a very deliberate thing and I was spared for a specific reason, probably to accomplish something in my life."

Doni C., 63, New Mexico, Restaurant Hospitality

The "Confederate Angel" is Doni's guide on a foggy night.

"ABOUT EIGHT YEARS AGO, I had a very interesting experience while driving a truck along an interstate in upper West Virginia on a foggy, foggy night. I was traveling north and taking my shift at the wheel while my husband Glenn slept in the bunk, and it was a struggle to keep going because it was impossible to see anything.

Suddenly, I heard a voice out of the dark, "Hey little lady, you doin' O.K. there?" I *hated* talking on the radio so I didn't respond. The strong, soothing voice filled my cab a second time, "C'mon little lady, talk to me so I can help you out." Finally I ventured, "You talkin' to me?" The friendly voice came back immediately, "Sure am! I can help you get through this bad patch here. I'll move on up and you pick up my taillights and we'll trailer it..." Shortly after that, another truck passed me and pulled over in front and I assumed it was the voice out of the dark. Suddenly the radio didn't seem so unpleasant, and I talked constantly with my "friend" for the next hour or two as we crept through the fog. Normally, when trucks are so close, they drown out others on the channel, but apparently no one heard us because no one cut in. My friend told me that his handle was "Confederate Angel."

Eventually, I said "There's my exit" and pulled off, just about the time Glenn was coming up to take over. He slipped into the seat and I told him what had been going on, and he wanted to try to catch up to the other truck. But even though we pulled immediately back onto the interstate on the ramp opposite and sped up, we couldn't see the truck, and the "Confederate Angel" didn't answer our call. Other truckers came on asking who we wanted, and we gave them his handle and *no one had ever heard of him*. Now this was odd, because he had told me that he pretty much only ran this same route through three states up and down this same freeway. *Someone* should have encountered him *somewhere*!

We asked drivers on that route often afterward if they had ever heard of a driver with that particular handle, and never found anyone who had seen or heard of a "Confederate Angel." As we thought about it, we realized that it was a pretty strange handle to pick because most of them are fairly raunchy, and no trucker had ever called himself an angel. Glenn and I became convinced that I had, in fact, met a REAL angel who had led me through the dangerous fog patch."

Juanita K., 67, Arizona, Ceramic Store Owner

A band of wily and treacherous bikers try to ensnare a senior couple, and on another occasion, a vicious storm parts before them like the Red Sea.

JUANITA HAS MANY STORIES of warnings and protection, and shared several of them with me. Her husband Grover has participated in most of these adventures with her, and both of them find it very easy to believe that someone watches over and protects them.

When Juanita had surgery in a hospital in Phoenix (about a four-hour ride from her home), she experienced a marvelous thing on her way back in the car. She was lying in a station wagon in which they had the back end open to allow air to blow through for cooling, and two of her children were holding down the sheet that covered her. About two-thirds of the way home, it began raining violently.

"As we left Wickiup, it started pouring and ahead of us was what almost appeared to be a huge black cloud covering the road. It looked so menacing that we talked about turning back and returning to Phoenix. However, I was in so much pain, and so desperate to get home that I urged Grover to keep driving and knew that God would help us through.

As we approached the area where the rain had turned the cloud to a black wall, it divided and opened up over the road. The darkness still appeared on each side of the road, but ahead of the car we had a clear path right down the middle. It felt very much like what the parting of the Red Sea must have been. We drove straight through the opening, and the cloud seemed to close behind us, because as we looked to the rear of the car, blackness covered the road again and a wall of water came gushing down.

The rain was so severe that the highway was washed out behind us and nobody else could get through. Ours was literally the last car that passed down that highway. It was scary approaching that dark cloud, but we truly believed that God would take care of us and we would be alright."

When Juanita went back for a second surgery, she had another dangerous encounter, this time of the human kind, as she returned home.

"As we drove down the highway, we saw a biker band—Hell's Angel types—with about 20 bikes parked by the side of the road, and two guys lying in the middle of the road. A third biker was trying to wave us over, presumably to help his fallen friends. As I saw them, I got a very bad feeling inside, and felt like I was being warned to immediately get away and not stop. The closer we came, the more intense the feeling was.

I told Grover to drive around them because I was becoming certain that they were going to harm us if we stopped. To them, it looked like he was slowing down, but suddenly he swerved and accelerated rapidly as he drove in a wide circle around them. When they realized what he was doing, we saw them scrambling for their bikes, including the two "sick" people who had been lying in the middle of the road.

Poor Grover floored that car and pushed it to the limits, and those bikers chased us for miles but couldn't catch us. They must have followed us for over 15 miles before giving up, and we were sure glad they went back because we had been afraid they would pursue us all the way home. We were very grateful when we saw them start to fade into the distance."

As Juanita concluded this story, Grover spoke up to verify that they indeed receive special help when they are out on the road. "When we are on trips, all of our car problems occur in town, and not when we are out on the road far from anyone and anything. Every time something goes wrong, there is help nearby. Even when we lost our transmission, it was five minutes from home on our return from a trip where we had driven thousands of miles."

Juanita had one more extremely unusual story to relate about something that happened after the death of her parents. Her father had always promised them, "I'll let you know somehow that your mother and I are together after we die, so you all will know we are O.K." Her father died first, and her mother died about two years ago. After the mother's death, their four children (Juanita was one of these) decided to go together to the family house to split up the belongings and remove what keepsakes they wanted.

"We went from room to room together looking at things…everything seemed to have a memory attached to it. In one room, we stopped at Daddy's old tie rack which had been recently refurbished and varnished by a brother-in-law. My sister decided that she wanted the stuffed snake that was draped over it, so I unwound it and handed it to her. Somehow, the snake fell to the floor, so I bent down and picked it up for her. As I passed it over, it fell again, only really it seemed to kind of "leap" from my hand.

This was so odd that all of us noticed it and everyone tried to pick it up for her, resulting in all of us bending over at almost the same moment to reach for that silly snake. As we did, a tremendous gust of wind came rushing through the house…so strong that some of the doors slammed and locked. The screen door into the kitchen, which had been locked, flew open and the regular kitchen door also blew wide open, but strangely enough to the outside, even though that door normally opens inward. We could look straight out through the bedroom and see that back door swinging wildly.

As we turned again to the tie rack, something strange had happened as that wind blew through. Just a moment ago, the newly varnished rack had been unblemished with a perfect, unadorned finish. Now, there appeared on the rack the symbol (one straight line with a second one slanted toward it) that my father had always used to mark his tools. That was his special, unique identification sign.

We stared in disbelief at the tie rack thinking that we were imagining this, but then realized that all of us couldn't be hallucinating. The mark looked something like chalk, but wouldn't rub off, no matter how hard it was scraped. To this day, it cannot be removed. We all believe that Daddy had somehow kept his promise to show us that he and mother were together, and this has given us comfort as time has passed."

Cindy J., 35, California, Utility Company
A car crashes through the busy front window of a crowded Post Office.

IN 1984, CINDY HAD BEEN WORKING at a new job for only two or three days when she was asked to go pick up the company's mail at a nearby Post Office. When she entered the lobby, more than a dozen people were waiting to be served, but Cindy noticed that they were all clustered into a corner on the left side near a wall. There were, in fact, diagonal ropes that marked lines in front of the counter, but no one was standing there.

Cindy hesitated momentarily, wondering if she should step forward toward the counter, or go stand with the other people since they clearly were ahead of her in line. Finally, she chose the more polite route and walked over to the far corner, joined the group of waiting people, and they moved only one at a time to the counter as a clerk became available.

Cindy had been standing there just a short time when suddenly a deafening crash shook the wall, glass shattered like confetti, and a car smashed through the front of the building. It slid across the lobby, directly through the roped lines scattering them like bowling pins, and hit the high counter with a terrible noise, finally coming to a shuddering stop. A woman parking her car had hit the gas pedal instead of her brake and crashed through the bay window on the front.

No customer happened to be standing in front of the counter at that exact moment, and all of the employees were protected by their counter. Not one person was injured! That certainly had to be a miracle in a busy Post Office first thing in the morning. Cindy said, "One of the employees told me that morning was different from all the others, that customers *always* stood in line between the ropes. If they didn't, the employees usually reminded them, but nobody had said anything to the customers yet.

For some unexplained reason, on this day only they were not standing where they were supposed to. I was particularly grateful, because I would have been at the end of the line, and the first person to be struck by the rampaging car. I know that people would have been injured or killed! The employee I spoke with said that she thought God had sent the angels to take care of all the people who were in the lobby that morning."

Kathy D., 34, Maryland, Accountant
Spinning wildly toward a narrow bridge, a young woman sees no room to pass a group of horrified, immobile pedestrians.

KATHY EXPERIENCED THE HAND of an angel on an icy, blustery winter day when she came within a hair's breadth of death. In 1989, a sudden and brutal February ice storm posed a problem for Kathy who needed to go to her job on a Saturday morning. "My boyfriend was really nervous about my being out on the roads and he asked me not to go. He was upset when I insisted that I needed to go anyway.

I went very slowly (it was worse than I thought it would be) but did fine until I got to a barren stretch of the Interstate where a car was stalled on a bridge. The traffic on that bridge had been reduced to just two narrow lanes because of construction. I was going maybe 40 mph as I approached the bridge and saw the stalled car, and when I tried to brake I started spinning out of control.

I headed straight toward a group of five young people who were trying to push the stalled vehicle and my heart almost stopped when I realized that I was probably going to hit them and couldn't do anything about it. I was close enough to see the frozen looks of terror on their faces too. I can't even describe what an awful feeling that was.

Suddenly, my car stopped spinning and slid backwards straight past the group with only a few feet to spare between the vehicle and the people standing there, and it began spinning crazily again as soon as it was past the group. I finally stopped in a swirl of snow about 30 feet on the other side of the bridge. For a moment, I just sat there numb, barely able to comprehend what had just happened, and when I could think clearly again, I realized the magnitude of what had occurred.

The thought that remains most clear in my mind is the distinct feeling throughout the entire incident that I *was not* the one in control of the vehicle. I know I did not execute that maneuver through some kind of extraordinary driving skill. I felt as if I was not alone, and the brief "Help me God!" prayer that I uttered had brought a heavenly messenger to my aid. When I tried to describe this later to my boyfriend, he seemed skeptical that I had received special protection from an angel, but regardless of what other people might think, I know that what happened was not typical or run-of-the-mill.

When I describe what I feel in my life now as a "consoling presence", that doesn't even do justice to the calm strength that seems to surround me. I have rediscovered my faith and my church, and live each day as a more aware human being cooperating with the work of God. My whole life is different because of that one incident. If you asked me if angels can make a difference to humans, my answer would be a resounding *yes*."

Dawn M., 35, Wyoming, Hospital Unit Secretary

A wind burst flips a Bronco, causing a nine-year-old to sustain a life-threatening injury.

"WHAT A GREAT WEEKEND we had had! We had been on a wonderful camping trip, and were returning home towing our 16 ft. camper trailer. We ran into some pretty heavy winds which can be quite dangerous in Wyoming, and soon were heading unaware toward disaster. At a point where the winds were the worst, the trailer started fishtailing and our camper just snapped off the back causing the Bronco to roll over. In fact, we rolled one and a half times forward with an impact strong enough to push us into a continuing roll two and a half times to the right side.

As we jolted to a dusty stop and a sudden stunned silence, we slowly looked around to count the kids and realized our nine-year-old daughter was missing from where she had been sitting in the back of the vehicle. All three back windows were smashed out and a horrified certainty set in... she had been thrown from the car...

My husband snapped authoritatively, "Stay here!" as he pulled himself out and staggered around the side of the Bronco. I didn't know at the time why he sounded so harsh and discovered later that highway statistics for rollover accidents show that often a passenger thrown from the vehicle will be underneath it. My husband was going out to look for what he thought was a dead daughter, and didn't want me to see her.

To his shock, our daughter was walking in a kind of dazed trance toward the crashed Bronco. About all she was able to moan was "Daddy..." before the whites of her eyes turned blood red and she slumped into a paralyzed heap.

The LifeFlight helicopter did come out, and they only really do that for life and death situations because by now we had a child who couldn't move a muscle. At the hospital, staff members were performing many tests because of the paralysis, and discovered that a ruptured pancreas was producing an incredible excess of the enzyme "amylase". The staff had scheduled blood transfusions, and the members of our church began praying earnestly and en masse.

Ultimately, it turned out that no transfusions were ever done because they became unnecessary. When my husband walked into the hospital room about four hours later, our daughter sat up, spoke, and hugged her dad, apparently able to function normally and no longer seriously ill. In fact, she was discharged from the hospital the next morning with her only residual injury being a small cut on her toe. Somehow, she had been cured of everything that was wrong with her, the amylase problem had disappeared, her system was cleansed, and the paralysis was gone.

One of the strangest discoveries of all, however, occurred when we later went back to the crash site and located my daughter's Bible which had been clutched in her hand as she was thrown from the car. It was approximately 30 feet away from where the vehicle had landed, and as we picked it up, we found *a huge, triangular shard of glass (probably 5 inches long) tucked neatly into the center of the Bible.*

Just thinking about how seriously she could have been injured from even that one piece of glass sent shivers down our backs. Clearly someone was taking extra-special care of that wonderful young lady to keep her from terrible harm, and we will always be grateful to her special protector."

Sandy J., 50, Arizona, Corporate Trainer, High Tech Industry
A last minute route change is crucial to avoiding an encounter with a flooded river.

"I HAD JUST MOVED to northeast Arkansas and had been living there for about three weeks when an extraordinary thing happened. I was preparing to leave the house one day when I received a call from my daughter at school, "Mom, I'm sick. Can you come and pick me up?" That call changed the course of the events that followed in a way that saved my life.

To go to the school, I chose a different route than the one I had intended to take for my errands. Either one of two roads would have taken me to the original destination I had planned before receiving my child's call: one ran alongside the levee that was holding back a flooded river that was at the 40-foot level, and the other did not go near the river, but was closer to the school.

The river road was the shorter of the two, and was the one I had intended to take. My daughter's call changed my plans, and so instead I took the road by the school to pick her up.

Near the cemetery before I even got to the school, the brakes on the van locked and I lost control of the car and rolled several times. The windshield popped out, but instead of flying out the front, I went into the back between the padded seats. During the time I was unconscious, I heard a very calm, soothing voice that said, "You're going to be alright. Don't worry." I was surrounded by a warm light while the voice spoke to me. This occurred before anyone arrived at the scene to help, so it was not a human voice encouraging me. Instantly, I knew that I would truly be OK despite having three broken ribs and being in shock.

What was most amazing to me was that, because of that one telephone call from my child, I had ended up driving on the road where I had the best chance of surviving. I had planned to travel on the shorter river road, and if the brakes had locked there, I would have rolled into the flooded river and drowned before anyone could get me out of the water. That one brief call changed my route and probably also the course of my life. I don't know how to explain this except that someone or something influenced it. I feel very fortunate for having been saved."

Linda W., 34, Indiana, Optician
A strong, sure voice tells Linda of an impending decision in the aftermath of a serious collision.

"IN 1980, I WAS DRIVING in extremely foggy weather with my younger brother who was at the wheel of the car. He missed a stop sign and caused an accident at an intersection. I hit the windshield with the most incredible force because seatbelts weren't as widely used then. As I woke up, I was pulling my face out of the shattered windshield thinking to myself, "Well, this wasn't so bad after all." You need to understand that I wasn't feeling any pain, but I could hear my brother crying out, "Oh my God, I killed her, I killed her..."

I heard very loudly and clearly a calm, low-pitched, incredibly resonant voice saying, "Don't worry, everything is being decided..." Somehow I understood that my earthly life was hanging in the balance, but I did not feel any kind of fear or apprehension. And I didn't feel any kind of pain either, just a calmness, and a sense of patient waiting. Suddenly I heard a second clear statement, "It has been decided."

At that second, I became aware of blinding pain and a gushing of blood from my face that was so profuse that it seemed as if someone had thrown a bucket of red stuff over my shoulder that flew out in front of me.

I spoke, and literally shocked my brother who was certain that I was dead; he had not expected me to revive. I ended up with fairly serious injuries, but everything was O.K. and I recovered just fine. I asked my brother if he had heard any voices or any sounds at all in the time immediately after the crash, and he assured me that he had heard nothing. Apparently, I was the only one who was aware of the "discussion" that was taking place about my life and was the only one who heard that firm, deep voice."

Bonnie K., 44, Arizona, Personnel
The wheels of a car miraculously straddle a deep well.

"I WAS VERY AWARE of being protected one time when I went to a car wash—one of the ones where you wash it yourself—and pulled into an empty bay. All of the bays have a steel grate in the middle covering a hole where the water goes down, and the opening under the grate is about 3 to 3 ½ feet deep.

As I went to step out of my car, I discovered that I had driven over a hole where the grate was missing and the opening was exposed. I had missed the opening by a fraction of an inch and was straddling the hole in a way that my wheels had not fallen down into the well. If I had driven into the opening, it would have been a terrible jolt, and probably I would have been injured as well as my car suffering damage.

I have always had a very strong attachment to angels, and feel that in this instance, I was very specifically aided by some who made sure that my car was positioned in a way where there was no danger. If I had driven in any other way than I did, it would have been a certain accident."

Mark R., 47, California, Health Care Administration
The enfolding arms of an angel save a trucker during a terrifying accident.

"I WAS A LONG-HAUL DRIVER for about nine years. On one trip, I was hauling radiators out of Fredericksburg, Wisconsin on highway 12, and because of the weight I was only going about 50 miles per hour in a 55 zone. I had a big string of cars behind me when I came to a county road crossing where there was a farm on the left-hand side close to the corner of the highway.

Out of the corner of my eye, I saw a car approaching the intersection and realized the car wasn't going to stop. I stood on my brakes really hard and started praying. It was too late, though. I went right up over the top of that car in my truck, mostly in the rear area. This next part is hard to describe, but as I was praying, I just felt something wrap around and embrace me with an enfolding that you could feel physically. Next thing I knew, I jackknifed that truck and went into a ditch by the farm.

I probably was out for awhile, but when I came to, there was a priest at the scene preparing to do the last rites, so I just stood right up and continued praising God with the prayer I had been praying when the accident happened. The priest was quite surprised and left to go over to tend the family in the car. When they examined us, I didn't have even a bump and one of the children in the car had a broken leg while the other had just a few minor cuts and bruises. However, no one was seriously hurt.

The driver of the car had not seen the stop sign and was responsible for causing the accident. But the police and doctors said it was an absolute miracle that there weren't fatal injuries and couldn't believe the mild nature of the actual injuries they treated. I'm not surprised, though! I believe that God protected us and kept us from harm. I am grateful for this miracle and try to live my life in a way that I deserve the blessings I have received."

A Most Unusual Kind of Protection…

When I was given my first story about someone being protected from danger by violating the laws of physical matter and *"passing through" another object as if they were both made out of air,* I was pretty skeptical but still intrigued. How could this happen? People and things are made out of physical matter, they have density…I can't just put my hand through a wall as if it doesn't exist! When several people recounted the same thing, however, "passing through" a car or a truck or a horse or a pole, I became more willing to accept that this could happen. I decided that just because I have never seen it doesn't mean it can't occur since there are people who have experienced it. Dorothy, Geri, Evelyn, David, and Joyce all somehow defied the laws of nature during their experiences, and I'm certain they are not inventing what occurred. You'll be as intrigued as I was. Here are their stories.

Dorothy S., 44, Arizona, Data Analyst

A couple pass through an accident as it happens on a busy freeway.

DURING A SUMMER around 1980, Dorothy and her family were on the way to a company picnic and were traveling in the center lane of I-17, the major arterial freeway at that time. All of a sudden, the two cars directly ahead of them in the center lane and the right lane hooked bumpers at full speed and Dorothy and her husband realized that an accident was imminent.

"My husband said, "Oh my God! We're going to hit them!" It certainly looked like we would crash within the next second. I blinked automatically for just a second, and when I opened my eyes, we were in front of the two cars with absolutely no idea of how we had passed them. I said to my husband, "My eyes were closed so I don't know how you did that, but it must have been a pretty incredible piece of defensive driving." He looked at me in shock and replied, "I don't know how I did it either, because what just happened here is physically impossible. *One second I was behind them and I could see a crash coming, and the next second I was in front of them!*"

The accident happened behind us and it delayed a lot of the people who were attending the picnic, because as they arrived, they were all complaining about the terrible tieup on the freeway, and how bad that accident was. I have no way to explain what happened to us, because as my husband said at the time, it seemed to violate any existing physical laws. Somehow, we just believed we had been saved from danger."

Geri P., 35, California, Real Estate

This young mother finds that her children's lives are saved as they passed through a huge truck blocking their lane.

"IN 1979, I WAS LIVING IN ANAHEIM, and was driving to my mother's in Victorville (about 50 miles away) after taking my husband to work. My two children were sleeping peacefully in the back of my hatchback car. I was driving in the fast lane against the median when up ahead I saw a semi-trailer that had detached from its cab and was stuck up against the median wall obstructing my lane. With horror I realized that my escape route in the lane next to me was blocked by a car traveling about the same speed I was, and apparently the driver was unaware of the potential crisis because he wasn't moving over to give me any room.

With only a short distance available to avoid an accident, I barely had time to glance in my mirror to see that my children were still lying down, utter a prayer, "God, please take care of my babies!", and think that at least they maybe had a chance to survive if we went under the massive truck since they were very low in the car.

My very next conscious thought was realizing that the lane ahead of me was clear and wide open, and I looked in my rear-view mirror to see that the semi-truck was still tight against the median wall blocking the lane I had been moving in. But this was all now *behind* me! And strangest of all, the car traveling in the lane next to me was still in the same position it had been before. That meant I had remained in my original lane. *Somehow I had simply passed through the truck as if my car was made of air.*

Although this sounds absolutely unbelievable, I know that the sequence happened exactly as I have described despite there being no explanation for how it could occur.

While I experienced a very real protection for myself and my children in the incident described above, I also have to mention a time that something else happened in our family. In 1974, when I was a teenager, my sister had a baby girl who was just two days old when she was saved from a sudden and horrible death. I was sleeping when I distinctly heard my mother's voice say urgently, "Geri, go get the baby." I remember thinking, "Why do you want me to go get her when I'm sleeping?"

However, I did do as I was asked: got up and and went into the baby's room, and picked her up out of her bassinet. Literally, less than a minute later, while I was still standing there next to the bed, a big ball from the outside came crashing through the window above the bassinet. A large, triangular piece of glass probably 2-3 feet long fell from the center of the window directly into the bed. The way it fell, it would have literally sliced the baby in half. The noise made the baby start to cry, and my mother who apparently was unaware of what had happened came into the room, saw me standing there holding my niece and said, "Geri, why did you wake the baby up?" I looked at her confused, "Because you told me to."

My mother declared, "But I never said anything to you! I knew you were sleeping." My mother was actually quite horrified when I showed her what had fallen in the crib. Neither one of us has any idea of where the voice came from that awakened me, but we have always believed that my niece had the special protection of angels."

Evelyn R., 29, Arizona, Computer Services
A professor and his wife see a car pass through their daughter.

EVELYN RECOUNTED THE STORY of a friend who has worked at least 20 years in a university environment: "My friend has always had a strong faith because he grew up Catholic and had a remarkable experience with one of his stepchildren when the child was really young. He always said it made him believe more firmly in the power of God.

His wife had two young daughters, so upon his marriage, he created an instant family. He worked in an office across the street from where his house was on campus. One day, as he walked out of his office, his five-year-old stepdaughter spotted him and started running across the street without looking. Her mother was standing on the lawn of the house but was too far away to help the child as a car drove straight toward her.

He stood frozen in horror as he and his wife both screamed in fear for their child. *The car passed right through the child who was unscathed and seemingly unaware of the incredible danger she had just escaped.* The car definitely did not pass beside the child because either one or the other of the parents would have temporarily had the child out of his or her line of sight. They each saw their daughter and the car simultaneously. He knows he didn't imagine it because when he compared notes with his wife, she had seen exactly what he had seen. He doesn't think they both could have hallucinated an identical event, and they were both always very grateful for the angelic rescue."

Evelyn's mother also told her a story about an event that she was too young to remember that happened to her as just a toddler in Okinawa, Japan. The storm screens on the house had been repaired after the winter, and had been leaned up against the windows prior to being securely refastened. Because the screen was loose, when Evelyn leaned against it, she fell face forward and head down out of the upstairs second floor window. When her mother ran in horror to the window, Evelyn was just out of sight below the window rim clinging to a gutterspout.

For a baby that age to have stopped her own fall, and turned around and caught hold of the spout was just amazing. Her mother always told her an angel must have plucked her out of the air and hung her on the spout until help could arrive.

David W., 44, Arizona, Library for the Blind

A car passes through a pole saving the lives of the passengers in a car.

"ONE TIME I WAS DRIVING to San Jose from the San Joaquin Valley with three other friends as passengers when we hit a water patch and went through some bad mud. The car was sliding and I wasn't correcting quickly enough, when we saw a pole dead ahead. We screamed and all had the sickening feeling that we were going to collide with it and there wasn't anything we could do about it. *The pole came closer and closer...and all of a sudden we were on the other side of the pole.*

We all saw this happen, and the only thing we could figure out was that we had passed right through it, which of course seems absolutely crazy. It wasn't something that only one person saw, so we know that we weren't nuts, but it is something that doesn't seem to make any logical sense. Of course, we were all grateful for being protected, even if we don't quite understand how."

Joyce W., 57, Minnesota, Accountant

The flooded road is blocked by monstrous Belgian horses and a family is suddenly on the other side of the animals.

"ONE TIME, MY HUSBAND AND I were driving to Hibbing, Minnesota through the McGregor Swamp on a very foggy night as often exists in spring and summer, and we happened to be passing through a particularly desolate stretch where there were no homes or farms nearby. Suddenly out of the fog, we saw two giant Belgian horses completely blocking the road, and we had absolutely nowhere to go to escape them, and not enough time to stop. Because of the size of these animals, a terrible accident seemed imminent, and either they or we would be injured seriously or killed.

We barely had time to realize the danger when we found ourselves on the other side of the horses and *they were disappearing into the fog behind our vehicle. Without them having moved, we seemed to have somehow passed through them.* Now that certainly defies all logical explanation.

One of our other Hibbing trips also brought us into contact with very dangerous circumstances. We were driving with three small children sleeping in the back of the car when we discovered that two of the highways ahead of us were flooded and only one was open. My adventurous husband muttered something like, "Well one road is all we need..." As we drove we were laughing that the last town we had to pass through was called Floodwood and how aptly named it was.

As we arrived there, humor was not really the right reaction because the water was already over the road, and yellow-coated emergency personnel were directing people across the flooded area. As we crossed and proceeded to the other side of town, we were getting into a place where there were no residences or buildings and the water was rising higher and higher. When our car stopped suddenly, we were pretty scared, but my husband dried off the distributor cap and we kept moving. Although we had no brakes after that, we somehow arrived safely at our destination. I just have to believe that we have been guided and protected more times than we can count.

One of the most dramatic times that sticks in my mind was when I was driving with a whole carload of people in South Dakota: a friend, her two children, and an elderly woman. It was night and we saw an approaching storm, noticing how beautiful the lightning configurations were. They were truly fascinating, but suddenly we saw that the lightning flashes were getting awfully close and we started to become a little frightened. We were in the prairie country where there wasn't much habitation, and certainly no roads to turn off on, only that one ribbon of freeway stretching out before us in the dark. We didn't have any choice except to just keep going.

I remember that we had been talking about angels when the storm seemed to overtake us and the car began to pitch about and just rocked from side to side. We realized now that the weather was worse than we had thought, and so we began to pray in earnest. The car seemed out of control, and we careened wildly around the highway. However, we somehow stayed on our path, and finally got to our destination, where I called my husband to tell him that we had arrived safely.

He said to me, "I'm so glad to know that you got in alright. We heard that there was a tornado on that highway, and we were all worried about you." I believe that we were kept safe on that highway in the middle of that storm by the angels who accompanied us and brought us to our destination."

LESSONS IN SERENITY

1. At a moment of great fear, if we release it and are open to a sense of calm and certainty that we will be taken care of, our fear will go away.

2. Sources of help will come in very unexpected ways. Instead of facing a situation where we expect the worst, if we project a conviction that we will be taken care, a sense of calm will fill us and help us through it.

3. In the world we live in every day, we need to develop a belief that we are not alone, and then our angel companions will help us in difficult situations, and we will live each day with a stronger feeling of calmness.

4. The moment that we begin to sense fear or nervousness inside, we need to focus our attention on consciously requesting assistance from angels rather than giving into and therefore increasing the fear.

PERSONAL JOURNAL

Think about the following, and record any impressions:

1. When did I ever have a feeling of anxiety or fear in a situation, and how did I resolve the circumstances? What helped me to achieve a sense of serenity and peacefulness?

2. Have I ever consciously asked my guardian angels to help me feel calmer and more in control?

INDIVIDUAL INSIGHTS OR OBSERVATIONS ABOUT "SERENITY" IN THE CIRCUMSTANCES OF MY LIFE:

Write in a journal any thoughts that come to mind.

Angels Who Teach and Guide

A Lesson in Hope

NE OF THE CONSISTENT STATEMENTS MADE by so many of the people I spoke with regarded "a little voice inside my head" that kept suggesting an action or decision or an answer in a time of confusion. People genuinely believe that there is a kind of guidance that comes from outside of themselves. Never did anyone say, "Well, I think I knew this all along, and it was really my own head talking to me." Instead, people are quite willing to accept the presence of what so many called their "guardian angel" and even seek out that voice by asking for its guidance.

It does not seem to be an abdication of responsibility to listen to advice from outside ourselves, but a comforting kind of reassurance that we are not alone, that there is someone else who cares about us and has our best interests at heart. Many who have not even sought information have found that these spontaneous and unsought internal "thoughts" and statements have been a rich source of direction and wise counsel.

The times when we are most confused and uncertain are the very times when we need to open our ears and eyes of faith, turn toward God, and ask for the comforting presence of the angels. Our despair can then turn into hope, and our uncertainty into wisdom.

Let's listen to some examples from people who firmly believe that they received guidance from their angels.

Mary W., 51, Michigan, Funeral Home Customer Service
A woman is guided off a busy freeway where she later learns a serious accident happened.

"TWENTY YEARS AGO, my husband, children and I were traveling home from a visit with our in-laws and we were on I-94, a very busy freeway. I suddenly began feeling an overwhelming urge to get off that freeway which could not be ignored, and when I tried to put my mind on something else it just kept getting stronger. I finally said to my husband, "Could we just get off 94 and go home on the surface streets?" He was puzzled and somewhat annoyed to have to take a longer way home, but gave in and did as I requested when I relayed how strongly I was feeling about this.

As soon as we left the freeway, I felt a little foolish but very relieved we were no longer on that road, and felt a huge sense of relief as if we had avoided some kind of terrible disaster. The rest of our evening was normal, and I thought no more about my strange experience...until the following morning.

After we got up, I said to my husband, "Grab the newspaper and see if you can find anything about 94, I still have this sense that something awful happened there last night." He was a little skeptical (probably thinking I had an overactive imagination) until he found the brief article. We were horrified to read that a family had been killed in a gruesome accident on a stretch of the road that we would have been traveling on at about that exact time of the disaster. I can't help but believe to this day that we were somehow steered away from potential danger."

Tory R., 42, Arizona, Police Department

Tory's instant lesson in controlling a vehicle on ice leads to a safe ending.

TORY SPOKE TO ME about her philosophy of living that was based on something she read years ago in a book: that she was supposed to keep herself constantly "in the presence of God." She refers to it as "practicing the presence." Tory says that for her, this is the only way to be guided to know whatever she needs to know at the moment. She related several examples of how knowledge came into her head that was something she did not know before that second.

"I was driving on a very bad, icy road one time in a 2-wheel drive vehicle and the freeway had a pretty steep slant at the place where I lost control of my truck. It spun around and I was going down the road backwards, which was terrifying for me since the diesel fuel that we carried in the back for emergencies started sloshing around. When I saw that I was headed directly for another car, and did not have control of my vehicle, I was afraid not only of a crash but of an explosion.

I prayed, "God what do I do here?" I received instant knowledge ...cramp the wheel this way, now hit the brake, now turn that way... Everything happened perfectly; the front swung around in the right direction, I avoided hitting the other car, and I slid easily (not slammed into) a snowbank and came to a gentle halt. All I had to do was calm down and stop shaking and I was ready to go on again.

A second time I remember was when I was trying to trim my horse's feet and had bought a book because I couldn't afford expensive groomers. The book described in detail what to do, but it didn't make sense to me, and I couldn't understand the directions. Plus, it scared me because the instructions stated that if you trimmed the wrong way, you would make the horse lame.

Again, I prayed for wisdom. "God, please help me understand these directions, you made this animal so it makes sense to you—show me what this means." Although I had never studied anatomy, I suddenly had a picture pop into my head that was a complete diagram of a horse's internal bone structure of the leg, and right then I saw why the book was right—that if I shifted the horse's weight because of the way I trimmed those hooves, it would affect the bones and throw the leg into an unnatural position. With that knowledge, I had no trouble following the directions and finished the job.

You can see that I have always felt guided and believe that whatever wisdom or knowledge we need will be given to us if we ask!"

Sheila R., 38, Texas, U.S. Military
An angel's guidance helps find the keys to escaping a potentially fatal situation.

ON A FRIDAY IN 1976, Sheila had gone to sign her papers to join military service. Coming out of the recruiting station in Brooklyn, she saw an old friend passing by whom she had briefly (but platonically) dated in school. Surprised to see each other, they chatted warmly about what had happened in each other's lives since they had last met. Sheila's friend suggested that he accompany her home to drop off the groceries he was carrying, and they would go get something to eat and spend time finishing the update.

"I felt perfectly comfortable agreeing to this. However, when we entered his apartment and a locking bolt automatically clicked in place behind me, I became slightly nervous when I looked around and saw how dirty and littered the efficiency unit was, and realized that a lot of the scattered magazines were pornographic. This was not the person I remembered. As he was putting the groceries away he offered me a drink, which I refused, but he took out a bottle of Jack Daniels and poured himself a huge glass anyway.

I was eager to leave for dinner and suggested this, but he sat there with his eyes getting wild, becoming quite agitated, and accused me of holding out on him while we had dated. When I told him I thought I should leave, he said I wasn't going anywhere, which struck fear into my heart. He then said that I could remove my clothes myself or he would tear them off because I wasn't going to get away from him again.

I asked to go into the bathroom (hoping there might be a window to escape) but realized when I got inside the tiny windowless room that I was completely trapped. I sat down and prayed, "Oh God, you have to help me here. I refuse to die like this. You must help me!"

Suddenly, he kicked the door open and pulled me out, crying, and I looked in shock at several plastic bags scattered open on the floor. One had a machete, one had an M16, and he screamed at me, "You're too stupid to get out of here, and you'll never live to tell anyone about this!" I was horrified beyond words.

He threw me down on the bed and began assaulting me, as I fought him furiously. I was unable to battle hard enough, and I suddenly heard a distinct voice saying to me intently, "Be calm...you will be alright." This startled me so much that I stopped struggling and listened. Again came the reassuring voice, "Tell him you like this." I was so dazed, I could hardly think. Tell him I liked it? What kind of crazy advice was that? Stumbling over the words, I did as I was told, and this seemed to calm him immediately. In fact, he rolled over and fell into a very heavy and deep sleep.

I grabbed my clothes and the M16 (I hoped it was loaded because I would sure aim and shoot if he came after me again...), headed toward the door and stopped short; it required a key to open that particular bolt. Oh no! I still couldn't escape because I was locked in!

This is where I know it had to be an angel voice that was guiding my steps. I heard that friendly voice slowly saying, "Stay calm. The keys are in the top drawer on the right side." There was only one chest in the room, so I ran over to it, frantically pulled open that top drawer, and sure enough, there was a huge ring with about a dozen keys on it. Momentarily I wondered, "What key do I need?" But somehow, the key with which I picked up the ring was the right one when I tried it in the lock. The cylinder clicked loudly, but as I glanced back, my attacker was almost comatose.

I ran into the alley, stopped to put my clothes on, and headed for a street with people on it. I raced up to a cab, and shouted, "Take me to the police station!" I think the poor cabbie first thought I was trying to rob him, because he looked bewilderedly at me brandishing the gun, but he did get me to the station.

The on-duty officer who would help me was on the telephone with a man who was reporting a robbery at his apartment, and as I listened, it turned out to be my "friend"/attacker. How dare he? I told them what had really happened, gave them the gun, and took them back to his apartment immediately. After they looked around and verified my story, they did arrest him and I pressed charges.

As I looked back on that event, I was always convinced that I received some angelic guidance at a time when I desperately needed it. I don't know how I would have found those keys in that crowded, littered apartment. The keys were what enabled me to get out of the situation without being injured or killed, and I have always been grateful."

Eileen C., 49, Wales U.K., Customer Service
A choir director is led to change her music…with interesting results.
"I HAD A VERY STRANGE EXPERIENCE recently with the church choir. We had just finished rehearsing particular songs for our Sunday service when I went home and my mind kept insisting that we do a different song. It was so strong that I rang the pianist and said that I had changed my mind and we would do this

other song. The new song is called "Put Your Faith in God" and is the story of Moses, David, Joseph, and Daniel.

That Sunday, it turned out that our visiting preacher was speaking on that exact topic and used the same four stories as illustration, so there was a perfect dovetail between the preaching and the music. That was very interesting to me."

"The most dramatic thing that ever happened to me in receiving guidance was what happened with my husband. In 1976, my husband had put in for and received a new job in South Wales and we were very uncertain that we were making the right decision to take this job and move. I had a friend at work who told me that in making decisions like this he always was guided by angels who helped him. I asked him if these angels of his might be able to tell us if we had made the right decision in taking the new job. He said, "They'll help you too…if you request it." So I asked for guidance.

Before I relate what happened next, let me explain that my husband had taken the new job temporarily and moved away, but I was still back at our previous house. I was finding this very hard emotionally, and was riddled with anxiety. One morning, my aunt arrived on my doorstep with this message: "I have a very odd thing to say to you. Ian's (my husband's) godmother received some kind of message that she seemed to feel was important. She was told to tell me to come to you and say that Ian made the right decision and everything is going to be alright. Do you know what this means?" I smiled broadly and told her that it made perfect sense to me even though I didn't offer to explain.

How could I tell her that I had asked angels about Ian's job decision? But I couldn't deny that she was standing there at my door with the very information I had sought. The comfort it gave me and the confirmation we had sought was very helpful in moving forward with confidence. History has shown that it was indeed the perfect step for both my husband and the entire family to take at that time."

Phyllis H., 40, Arizona, Engineer
An unseen guide shows Phyllis the only position that can save her baby.

"ELEVEN YEARS AGO, I was pregnant with my first child and about a month before I was due, my obstetrician said that the baby might come a little early. "How early?", I asked. "I'll be better able to tell you on your next visit" was the reply. The *next day* I went into labor!

I was alone at the time and found that the only position in which I was comfortable was to be on my hands and knees. Finally, my husband arrived to take me to the hospital, but again I got into the back seat and had to be on my hands and knees. Even at the hospital it was taking forever to get checked in and I felt like I wanted to get down on my hands and knees. People found it very strange that I kept reverting to this unusual position.

When I finally was placed in a room at the hospital, they found that I was 10cm dilated and the baby was breeched. My baby was ultimately successfully delivered but I read later in a book about home delivery that the birthing mother is to assume a position on hands and knees if the baby is breeched. To be in any other position, the baby would have been seriously harmed by potentially having its air supply cut off.

I was surprised that kind of information wasn't made a part of things like my LaMaze class. I had never learned of it there. Some kind of protective force had guided me and given me knowledge that I desperately needed to save my baby, and thanks to that, I had a healthy child. I will always be grateful."

Paulette P., Arizona, Consultant
After a night of suicidal thoughts, Paulette is guided directly to the people who will help her into treatment and a new life.

"MY LIFE TODAY IS COMPLETELY SURROUNDED by the presence of angels from whom I receive continual guidance, but it took some traumatic experiences to accept this. Once I lived a very high profile, high achievement life as a successful television producer on PBS. Other people even admired me as a role model, but inside I felt that I had become "spiritually bankrupt." I had developed a chemical dependence problem, started going into a downward spiral and ultimately arrived at the point of contemplating suicide.

One night I got to the point where I just *knew* I was going to kill myself and it was the most terrifying feeling. Voices inside kept saying, "Hang on just until dawn and you'll make it." That became like a lifeline; the knowledge that if I could wait until daylight I might be able to live. Slowly a conviction grew: "If I make it through this night, I will survive."

So I decided that dawn was a goal; I walked and walked and walked just to keep my legs moving. As light grew in the sky, I got into my car and started driving with tears blinding my eyes. What were those tears? Relief? Hope? Sadness that I still had to find a way? Grief? Eventually, I ended up in the rush hour traffic, just flowing with the moving vehicles, no destination in mind, no goal, no sense of where I was or where I was going. I seemed to hear a guiding voice: turn here, turn there, go right, go left and I blindly followed the silent directions, numb and empty-feeling. When I stopped, I looked up and saw that I was at the offices of John Bradshaw in Houston.

I walked inside with a feeling that someone else was guiding my footsteps, and found a bustling office. Someone took me into a side room and spoke with me and the next thing I knew, they had a treatment center in Arizona on the line. I immediately went into the program and ended up staying about a month, although I initially felt somewhat embarrassed and ashamed to be in what I considered a kind of "nut-house".

After several weeks, when I had already confronted many of my demons and had begun to look at life with a renewed sense of hope, I had a wonderful vision. It was a beautiful lady, a spirit of light with a white and gold glow around her. She placed hands very gently upon my shoulders and said, "You need to understand that those of you who are here right now will lead the way for others." I began to feel as if there was a reason for some of the suffering and learning that I had struggled through, that I would in some way help others grow and learn.

A purpose began to build within me and it has only grown stronger and stronger. I have devoted myself to listening to and understanding spiritual things which has brought so many wonderful gifts into my life."

Molly L., 23, Minnesota, Veterinary Technician

A grieving widow finds her husband's insurance papers in a most unusual way.

"IN APPROXIMATELY 1974, when I was very young, my grandfather died suddenly from a stroke, and shortly afterward, the family was gathered in the kitchen. His wife (my grandmother), daughter (my mother), son and daughter-in-law were all sitting together talking about where the insurance papers were stored. My grandmother didn't know where to look, and said, "I wish I could find Ray's insurance papers." My mother was sitting in grandpa's big leather chair in front of a china cabinet where beautiful antique hand-painted plates were stored, a spot where they had resided for over twenty years.

Suddenly, one plate flew off the cabinet, sailed over my mother's head and landed at her feet. The miracle was that it did not break, as fragile as it was. As she picked up the plate to safeguard it, my mother happened to open a drawer in the china cabinet where they saw papers, and after going through them, discovered the missing insurance documents.

Another unusual thing happened right around that same time. For the next couple of nights, both my grandmother and one of the granddaughters heard footsteps walking through the house, and the sounds of change jingling in a pocket. It was so vivid that they both got up and looked for my grandfather, but of course didn't see anything."

Janet M., 48, Indiana, Financial Industry
A heavenly sign shows Janet that things will be alright.

IN 1993, JANET WAS GOING THROUGH a very painful and acrimonious divorce. At the point where she had sold their house, she didn't know if there would be enough money to put down on a house of her own for herself and her three children. The legalities of the property disposition were very much up in the air.

"I was deeply depressed and just didn't see my way through all of the difficulties I was facing. As I was driving, I begged God for some kind of physical sign, something that would tell me that I would be able to get through all of my problems. I turned a corner and there in front of me was a *huge rainbow* which seemed to be *directly over my house*. In my heart, a sudden peace and strength assured me that everything would be O.K.

The next day, the papers indeed got processed despite three different cancellations or postponements by my ex-husband's attorney. The final closing was such a relief to me, but through that whole day I just had a firm conviction that everything would turn out alright. Ever since then, no matter what happens to me—through troubles with my children, or personal doubts and dark days—the memory of my special rainbow always sustains me. Every day that I recall its timely appearance, I smile and know with certainty that things will work out for me."

*   *   *

Another example of how a physical sign can be tremendously comforting when we are in the midst of worry, doubt, or confusion is shown in a story from Cyd.

Cyd D., 41, Indiana, Librarian
Cyd is comforted in her distress about a sister's troubled pregnancy.

"ALTHOUGH I HAVE ACTUALLY HAD many times when I have experienced comfort when I was sad or worried, one time sticks out in my mind. I was leaving work and headed home and I was thinking about my sister, in fact I was terribly worried about her. She was pregnant and had lost 30 pounds so far in the pregnancy, and everyone was very worried about the health of the baby. The doctors were discussing options that were fairly severe, and I just couldn't get her off my mind as I walked home from work that day.

I was going through a field near my house and praying intently for my sister and the baby when I happened to look up into the *cloudless blue sky* and saw *two rainbows*. It was the most incredible thing to see that in a sunny sky, and one rainbow was directly over my house while the other one was over my sister's house. At that moment, I knew with a calmness and certainty that my sister and her baby would both be just fine. And that is exactly how things turned out.

One other time when I was on vacation in the Upper Peninsula of Michigan, and very concerned that a mortgage that was awaiting approval wouldn't go through, I again saw that comforting rainbow in the clear, blue sky. When the sign appeared, I believed that my worries were groundless and the mortgage would be approved.

I called the mortgage company when I got back home, and they said that although they had thought that further documentation would be needed, they had decided that it was fine and had approved the loan. That approval had been given on the very day I had seen my reassuring rainbow. I honestly believe those signs were given to me to strengthen my faith and offer me hope. In each case, the reassurance was so powerful that I just would not give into worry and despair."

LESSONS IN HOPE

1. When we are not sure in what direction our life is going, or cannot see our way along a path, that is not the time to despair or allow discouragement, but the very time to look for guidance and renew hope.

2. The source of inspiration and optimism can come from very unlikely sources: through other people, from external signs, from soft inner leadings, by apparently "fortunate" circumstances, by doors seeming to open in front of us.

3. When we follow the guidance and direction that we receive, things always work in our favor, or to our advantage, and we are better off for having listened.

4. Hope is to share. When we receive this very special gift, we should pass it on by encouraging others and acting as a source of enthusiasm to spark their feelings of optimism.

PERSONAL JOURNAL

Think about the following, and record any impressions:

1. At a time in my life when I was discouraged, distressed or confused, did I look to God and the angels for comfort and hope, or did I encourage feelings of despair, and welcome doubt?

2. Where I did pay attention to guidance I received, what happened in my own personal circumstances?

3. What special people, situations, or signs gave me specific feelings of optimism? Did I ask for these, or receive them unbidden?

INDIVIDUAL INSIGHTS OR OBSERVATIONS ABOUT "HOPE" IN THE CIRCUMSTANCES OF MY LIFE:

Write in a journal any thoughts that come to mind.

Angels Aid Children and Families

A Lesson in Joy

GOD TAKES SPECIAL CARE OF CHILDREN

OD SEEMS TO HAVE a special protection for children and often sends the angels to save them from harm. The traditional pictures of small children walking with angels hovering over their shoulders probably best depict the spiritual reality that occurs when children are in danger. It is the children who have an openness to wondrous things that adults want extensive explanations and proof for.

In an example from the newspaper headlines, a recent crisis at a California school resulted in a most phenomenal occurrence for the children who were involved. I spoke with a woman whose child was in the classroom where a man with a gun was holding the class hostage. While the media did not report this to the public, the children revealed to their parents that there were numerous men and woman dressed in white who were fluttering around them at the time when they were in danger. The children, of course, had absolutely no trouble accepting the fact that angels might have been there to protect them. It was the adults who said that the stories were the result of fanciful imaginings created by fear and stress! However, those who know that angels are very close to children have no problem at all believing that they were being protected by hovering helpers.

All of the stories in this chapter are heartwarming examples of how precious little people were not alone when they needed assistance, or how family members were aided. The first story unequivocally shows that an angel will be nearby when a child needs special help.

Diana C., 48, Michigan, Food Processing Industry
A car is inexplicably moved out of the path of a bewildered three-year-old.

"IN 1974, MY SON WAS 9 YEARS OLD and my daughter was 3 years old. We lived on a very busy street and I had quite strict rules about the children playing outside or near the street. One of our fears was that the neighborhood children were in danger from the often-speeding automobiles roaring past our homes. Even though posted limits existed on our street, they were violated so often that they might as well not even have been there at all.

One day I looked out the front window and saw my youngest child Jeannie and several other children playing across the street despite my repeated requests not to cross that road. Going outside I called to them to wait for me to come over and get them. As I walked across the lawn my daughter looked up and saw me, and probably motivated by guilt, decided to quickly get back on her own side of the road.

She started running toward me into the street as I looked to the right in horror and saw a speeding vehicle bearing down on her. I remember screaming "Oh my God, God help her, please God!" The driver was caught in a very difficult position because there were other cars coming in both directions and children on both sides of the street. He didn't really have any way to go without hitting someone or something, and at this point, I was close enough to see the look of frozen shock on his face.

All of a sudden, his car veered sharply to the right directly into an empty driveway! Jeannie's momentum carried her into the car very slightly, but it was merely a bump that knocked her down and didn't do any damage of any kind. The visibly shaken driver jumped from his car explaining that he was hurrying to get his pregnant wife who was in labor to the hospital to deliver their child and he was sorry to be driving so fast through our neighborhood. He also volunteered something else that seemed to seriously puzzle him: as he approached the children, his hands were paralyzed on the steering wheel and he didn't know where to turn that someone inside or outside of his car wouldn't be injured. He feared for the safety of his wife and unborn child and for all of the children on the street, especially my daughter. All of a sudden, *the steering wheel moved under his rigid fingers without his controlling it in any way*, and turned the car so that the children were not hurt. It was also the safest thing for his own family to ensure they weren't hurt. He said with quiet conviction, "I know I didn't do this—someone else had control. I just couldn't have done it...I didn't even see that driveway!" He quickly continued on to the hospital and I hugged my daughter tightly knowing beyond a shadow of a doubt that an angel had placed wings around her and saved her from harm. She didn't have a scratch but I certainly had a renewed faith since God heard that urgently uttered prayer and stepped in to send a protector."

Pete S., 33, Arizona, Computer Industry Marketing Manager
As a van strikes a child riding a bicycle, the boy is found standing on the sidewalk unhurt.

THE EIGHT-YEAR-OLD SON OF PETE'S MINISTER had an extraordinary experience on a friend's bicycle. He wasn't completely familiar with the bike so he was less comfortable than with his own, and was not in complete control as he approached an extremely busy road in Chandler. A van veered in the path of the bicycle, which was struck and completely demolished, but the young boy was unharmed. Not only did he not have a scratch, but at the moment the bike hit the vehicle he wasn't even astride it, instead standing upright on the sidewalk. He told his father: "I felt a huge hand lift me right off that bike." No matter how unusual that sounded, he refused to change his view of the event in any way, and remained convinced that a hand had saved him.

Craig P., 35, Arizona, Quality Assurance Inspector

A cure for a baby that has no explanation but a miracle.

"WHEN MY DAUGHTER CHELSEA WAS ONLY 14 MONTHS OLD, she was diagnosed with leukemia at Children's Hospital. This was just devastating since her blood cells were 96% covered with the leukemia cells and there didn't appear to be much hope for survival even with treatment.

They admitted her to begin chemotherapy and we, of course, all began praying. Less than a week later, before the treatment course had even started, one of their final tests showed no evidence of the disease. Chelsea was leukemia-free! They did some treatment anyway, just to guarantee the leukemia was gone, but our explanation for it was the hand of God in the form of a miracle."

Yonette (Yoney) C., 31, California, Travel Consultant/Business Owner

Yoney's underwater vision may have saved her life.

"WHEN I WAS JUST FIVE YEARS OLD, I was camping with my family and some family friends at a big lake when something terrible happened while my father was out hunting. The son of my father's friend pushed me into the water, and since he was mildly retarded, he probably didn't understand that I was in trouble and needed help. I was actually drowning, but had the strangest experience under the water.

I saw two men with me, and felt very calm and didn't panic. It didn't seem awkward or unusual to see them, and they did not speak to me, just looked at me with very gentle expressions as we floated. It just seemed friendly and nice, and their faces reminded me of my father and my brother.

Suddenly, my father's friend pulled me out of the lake, and my mother was screaming hysterically. I choked and gasped somewhat, but remarkably had swallowed very little water, and suffered no after-effects. I have felt very special my entire life, because even though I was too young to truly understand what had happened, I knew that somehow I was different."

Mary V., 27, Arizona, University
A vision in the night reveals to a frightened young couple that their baby is alive and healthy.

"WHEN I WAS PREGNANT WITH OUR FIRST CHILD IN 1982, my husband and I were very young and we were struggling financially. Every day we ate rice and beans, rice and beans... It was very hard to find food and shelter, and my baby really did not receive the right kind of nutrition which worried me greatly. Sometimes we would walk through the neighborhood and eat oranges and grapefruit from the trees of kind neighbors who had allowed us to share their harvest. Through the first several months of the pregnancy, however, I lost over 30 pounds.

At five months, the baby still had not moved, and because I had not been going to the doctor, I was worried that my baby was not healthy. I shared my fears with my husband and he was sympathetic. One night, I was praying before I went to sleep, "Oh God, please help this baby be O.K.; I am so afraid."

During the night, I awoke one time to see a very bright light building in intensity within the room. It was much more intense than light from lamps or bulbs. The light seemed to move toward the bed and concentrate right behind the bulge of my abdomen. At the same moment, I was feeling an overwhelmingly warm, comforting feeling and I was not at all frightened by what was happening.

My stomach began to glow and the light was coming from behind so that it seemed as if my womb became transparent. I could see the outline of a tiny head and face and miniscule hands pressed against the inside of the womb the way one might press their hands against a window with fingers outstretched. A tiny mouth was open in the shape of "ah." Through all of this I could not physically move but I was definitely aware of the room and the walls and all of my surroundings. After the light faded, I drifted off to sleep with a feeling of peace and calmness that had not existed before.

The next morning I was torn . . . should I mention this to my husband or keep silent? Would he think such an occurrence so strange that he would say I was crazy?

Tentatively, I spoke. My husband listened intently as I started to tell him what I had seen. He interrupted me and described what he thought had been a dream, but it was exactly what I had experienced. We couldn't both have had an identical dream! At that moment, we were a little in awe that we had received a message from God, but we were absolutely certain that our baby was safe and healthy.

Shortly afterward, the baby did move and kick at six and a half months. However, we really didn't even need that to happen to know that she was doing fine. When she was born, we called her Angel Marie, and it has been a most fitting name. This young girl has a loving, caring, sensitive personality. Just as we knew when that heavenly light came into our bedroom the night we needed reassurance, everything did turn out just fine."

David and Marie M., Arizona, Public Service
Ryen's contact with the angels affects the whole family.

"OUR SON RYEN, who is now 9 years old, survived a very challenging infancy. He was hospitalized at four days old with a non-functioning liver but pulled through. As a young child, a friend threw a lawn dart at him, which hit him in the cheek instead of damaging his eye. So we have always known that he is special.

When Ryen was about three, he came to us and said "Why don't we go to church? These angels came to me and said they knew who I am and I am supposed to help our family get stronger." When we quizzed him about these "angels", he told us that they spoke with him and wore red robes, and came in through his window. Ryen told us they had said he should go to "God's school", so we in fact did place him in a private, parochial school where he has done very well. And as promised, our whole family has grown together and become stronger because of the influence of Ryen and his angels."

Traci J., 22, Iowa, Office Systems Sales
A brilliant figure cures a seven-year-old's irrational fears.

"I HAVE ALWAYS BELIEVED IN ANGELS participating in people's lives ever since my mother told me this story about something that happened to her as a little girl. Her mother (my grandmother) died when my mom was seven years old, and this triggered a lot of somewhat irrational fears in her that stayed with her. She was afraid of being alone and afraid of the dark, and in fact just began developing a very timid demeanor in general.

One time, she was alone feeling particularly fearful and a huge figure appeared in her room that was so transparent that she could see through it and it was made of a brilliant white light. The figure exuded strength and love, and held out its arms. She didn't hear actual words, but had a very strong feeling that seemed to say, "You'll be just fine. I'm here to protect you." Such a wonderful feeling accompanied this apparition that my mother lost all of the fears that she had been developing and was no longer afraid of anything, including the dark."

Regina B., 31, Arizona, University Administration
A daughter's dedication is rewarded in a most special way.

"IN 1944, MY GRANDFATHER, who was a small shopkeeper in East Germany, was taken away with no warning by the Russians and was not heard from again. When this sort of thing happened during that time of war, the family always knew that the prisoner had been killed, and my mother's family indeed believed their father was dead as the years passed with no further word.

But my mother, who was just eight years old when her father disappeared, refused to believe that her father was gone, and kept telling family members that he was alive somewhere. She ended up shouldering much of the responsibility for the family because her mother (my grandmother) could not bear the strain of losing her husband and became an emotional wreck, unable to function very well.

My mother so strongly believed in the return of her father that she would periodically go to the train station and wait through the arrival and departure of many trains searching the face of each passenger for the beloved parent. She just never lost hope!

Eight years later, when my mother was sixteen, she had an intense feeling on Christmas Eve that my grandfather would be returning home. There was nothing to indicate that this day was any different than the almost three thousand days that had preceded it except for that calm inner certainty that said, "This is the day." As my mother told various family members about her conviction that father would be at their table that Christmas Eve, they in turn scoffed at and then berated her for continuing to believe an idea that was nothing but empty hope.

As she went to the basement level where the store was below the house to pick up an item needed for their dinner, she was startled to see a shadow fall across the door and then a knock. With fast-beating heart my mother looked out the glass to a strange yet familiar face...her father, who indeed had returned home. The empty place in their family had been filled again.

He never was able to tell them where he had been or what had happened to him because of threats by the government which they all took very seriously. They knew it must have been terrible because of the nervous backward glances, sudden startled looks, and mostly quiet, sad demeanor that grandfather exhibited. Despite all that, there was a profound joy to have him home again, and the family accepted that they would probably never completely understand everything that he had been through."

Regina has a marvelously interesting postscript to this story as she tells what happened after her grandfather settled in upon his return. "When grandfather came back, they pretended to act like a normal family, but slowly and secretively made plans to escape from East Germany. We did not want to run the risk that anything like this could ever happen to our family again.

Very, very carefully each tiny step was put into place: money was sent to various relatives in small amounts to be placed into an account for the family, they went on visits across the border into West Germany taking a few personal belongings each time which were then left behind to be stored for their arrival. The saddest part was deciding what to leave behind, which was really a tremendous amount.

When the actual time for the departure came, there were six of them: two parents and four children, one boy and three girls (one of which was my mother). Although my mother had made several trips over the border smuggling jewelry, money, and heirlooms to other family members on visits, she had told me that there was something quite different about leaving for good, and she was frightened.

The family had to pretend that they were coming back by traveling on different trains rather than together as a group. My grandparents, their son and the youngest daughter had taken the early train, and the remaining two girls, including my mother, were to take the later train. Hours later, there they were in the very back of the last train car, sitting near an older couple as they had been instructed so it would appear to a casual observer that they were chaperoned. And this "appearance" was important since perception was everything in this type of situation.

Near the border, a soldier entered the car and began checking papers starting at the front, something that was done on a random basis. My mother and her sister froze…they had one-way tickets and if their documentation was checked they would surely be taken away and interrogated and probably arrested.

They began praying silently for help clutching each other's hands. When the soldier was just two seats away, the train jerked and started to move and the soldier shrugged his shoulders, looked at the last couple of seats and decided not to take the time to check since he had to hurry to get off before the train picked up too much speed. He turned and left without any further glance in their direction.

My mom and aunt went weak; they were going to be spared. My mother tells me that when they finally arrived at freedom, they collapsed to the ground and kissed it. Only my mother later left West Germany and came to the United States in 1960, while the rest of the family members made a happy life in the freedom of West Germany.

And by the way, even after he was out of the clutches of the East Germans, my grandfather never did speak again of the lost years in captivity."

Was it just a coincidence that the train began to move as the soldier approached the two frightened, young girls or had they indeed received the heavenly help they had requested?

Shary O., 52, Arizona, Teacher/Counselor for cancer patients
Shary is blessed with the ability to hear a heavenly chorus.

"ONE NIGHT MY LEGS WERE HURTING SO BADLY. I fell asleep finally, but awoke when I felt someone gently rubbing my legs, the most lovely and gentle touch…very comforting. I thought for a moment I was imagining this, but after looking twice, I'm certain I saw a dark-haired woman sitting at the end of my bed. Could this have been my mother who had been dead for many years? She had dark hair and had been a nurse. What a wonderful experience to be visited by someone you love so much.

The only incident that could eclipse this for me was the most incredible thing that occurred at a religious camp I attended for seven days on Mingus Mountain. What I experienced had never happened to me before that, and has never happened again since. At the camp, while we did our early morning meditation, I used to sing quietly for the group.

One morning, I was singing a lovely hymn, and came to the words, "…the presence of Jesus is in this place…", and as I sang, the air seemed suddenly filled with a thousand symphonies and ten thousand Tabernacle Choirs. It was more glorious than words can describe as the very air reverberated with energy, aliveness, and melody.

My eyes flew open, and I looked around to see if others were marveling as I was, but they all were peacefully meditating, and seemed unaware of the momentous event. That must have been the celestial chorus that we read about in the Bible. I had always wondered about that music of the angels, and why no one but the shepherds were able to hear it. In the Bible, the way it is written, you would think that the whole world would be deafened by the glorious songs.

The memory of that one event has always been very precious to me, and while I may never in my life hear this again, that one time was enough for me to hold in my heart."

Carla K., 46, Arizona, Equal Opportunity Officer
A subtle message saves a family heirloom.

"BECAUSE MY MOTHER PASSED AWAY while she was visiting in Illinois, we buried here there and later had to clean out her apartment in Arizona. My sisters and I worked very hard sorting things into piles that would go to the various families, things that would be donated to charity, and discards. After a long day, we finally went to bed. I couldn't go to sleep and decided it was because I was stressed and overtired. All at once, I "felt" my mother's voice: "Carla, you're missing something; go back and check again, look behind everything, pull out drawers, don't leave anything behind."

I couldn't sleep anyway, so I went out and walked back and forth among the various piles trying to decide what it was that my mother was trying to tell me. Nothing seemed to click with me until I found myself passing again and again the same shelf with a discard pile on it. I looked closer and finally picked up an object that I couldn't stop looking at. It was a carved pedestal with a rack on the side to hang spoons and a flying bird on the top. It was black and stained which was probably why someone threw it in the junk pile.

I took some silver polish and began to work on it, and found a real treasure under the grime. It was a pure silver antique soup server that we later learned had belonged to our grandfather's family in Russia in the 1800s.

I believe that my mother wanted this heirloom to remain in the family, because I had a very good feeling as I was lovingly polishing it. My mother and I were the ones who used to go antiquing together and it was a really special bond between us. I think that she didn't want her precious antique to be lost."

Kathy H., 50, Arizona, Executive Secretary/City Management
A beloved son's tender goodbye... only slightly delayed.

IN JUNE 1992, KATHY'S 25 YEAR-OLD SON died suddenly and she was grieving terribly. One time, after a visit from her daughter, she was lying on a loveseat absently watching television while her husband sat nearby on a couch. Kathy was extremely tired but unable to sleep, and the harder she tried, the more elusive sleep seemed.

As she drifted in a kind of "twilight zone", she was thinking of her son, feeling very lonely and missing him dreadfully. Suddenly, she felt the gentlest of touches—a slight brush against her bangs as if a delicate hand had smoothed her hair and a wisp of a kiss softly caressed her cheek, startling her. "I called to my husband, "Al, did you just come over and kiss me?" but he said that he hadn't moved. I had the strongest sense that my son was present in the room and was assuring me that he was alright and that I could let go of my overpowering regret. The regret stemmed from the fact that I had been unable to tell him goodbye because he had died while we were on vacation. What a lovely way to resolve some of my feelings of incompleteness, because I think he was trying to reassure me."

From an article printed in the Catholic Voice, Archdiocese of Omaha, written by Ron Green, November 12, 1993, reprinted with permission

SCENE ONE: PENNELLVILLE, N.Y., AUGUST 1961

We had just finished eating Sunday dinner. The lady who in six days would become my mother-in-law, Marjorie O'Brien, was returning to the table with a cup of coffee when the old grandfather clock chimed. This clock had come down the Erie Canal on her father's boat and had sat in this kitchen for years—without chiming. Marjorie dropped her cup on the floor and exclaimed, "My God!" She then crash-landed into her chair looking as if she had seen a ghost; for good reason, it turned out. After catching her breath and regaining her composure, this woman who normally leaned in favor of skepticism very matter-of-factly told us: "I just saw my Mother (who was deceased) walk through that doorway. She had come to wind the clock. She always wound that clock on Sundays."

SCENE TWO: I-84, COLUMBIA RIVER GORGE, MARCH 1982

Marjorie had just died. Dawn had flown to Oregon City to be with her father and brothers. Our six children and I were driving nonstop from Casper, Wyoming. My oldest son had taken the wheel at about 2 a.m. and I was asleep when suddenly someone spoke to me, and awakening I found our Dodge van heading straight for a concrete wall. My son, the driver, had also gone to sleep. I grabbed the wheel and we escaped with only badly mashed hubcaps. As you may understand, I decided to finish the drive into Oregon City, but as I sat there behind the wheel, now fully awake, I thought back to why it was that I awoke. And, if I had had a coffee cup in my hand at that moment, I too would have dropped it. The voice I had heard, the voice that said, "Ronnie!" was Marjorie's voice. She had been one of the few people to continue calling me by that name. Certainly no one in the van that morning had ever referred to their dad as Ronnie. And so, when we arrived at our destination, I put my arms around Lee and said "Well, Pop, the Old Lady has already checked in and been sent out on an assignment!"

SCENE THREE: OUR LIVING ROOM, NOVEMBER 7, 1992

Dawn had died early in the morning. It was now evening and I was seated on the couch where Dawn normally had positioned herself. I was reviewing her journals looking for excerpts to read at her wake as she had requested. I found a particularly interesting passage—a premonition of dying. I moved a book off "Dawn's seat" so Kelly could sit by my side to also read Mom's prophetic call, and when I did so a Christmas ornament hook jabbed into my finger. Since there was no earthly explanation for the hook to be in that place at that time, we both knew then that Mom wanted to remind us that the annual family Christmas name drawing had not been brought to completion before she left; that it was important to her that we continue the longstanding family tradition even in her absence.

LESSONS IN JOY

1. The most beautiful angelic interactions affect innocent ones such as children, who are so trusting and accepting. They do not try to explain or analyze a gift from an angel, but simply believe with a pure joy and a welcoming attitude. The children are good role models for the adults.

2. While an angel presence may not be as obvious when we are interacting with family members, sometimes events appear to be influenced so that the family can be there for each other when they are needed.

3. The delight that children take in being surrounded by angels is a source of joy and inspiration for all who see it. Everyone can grow by observing and learning from it rather than scoffing at it.

4. We can look for opportunities in our own lives where we are led to help friends and family members and be attentive to how we can offer them joy. It is possible that we are being led by the angels to make this happen.

5. Our greatest lesson is to rediscover and embrace the pure joy, freedom, and innocence of the child within us.

6. The uncensored response of innocence is an empowering freedom for adults.

PERSONAL JOURNAL

Think about the following, and record any impressions:

1. Has there ever been a time in my own life when I felt that unusual circumstances were prompting me to be somewhere or do something that was needed in my family? What was the result of that?

2.   As a child, did I ever feel a special presence or receive even in a small way some sense that I was not alone? Was I ever comforted in distress or fear even if an adult was not around? Did I ever see or hear something that other people thought was not real or told me had not really happened? Did I feel happy when these happened? How did I feel?

3.   As an adult, have I ever been able to let go of the inhibiting belief system instilled by the socialization process, and feel a pure freedom inside?

INDIVIDUAL INSIGHTS OR OBSERVATIONS ABOUT "JOY"
IN THE CIRCUMSTANCES OF MY LIFE:

Write in a journal any thoughts that come to mind.

Angels Help Us Receive Messages in Dreams

A Lesson in Belief

I HAD NOT ORIGINALLY INTENDED to write anything about dreams—it did not seem to necessarily apply to my topic of encounters with angels. However, I noted an intriguing pattern recur as people spoke of things that happened to them or messages that they received while they were sleeping. When I realized that often the information they were receiving could not have come from any source that was part of their own experience and knowledge (i.e. their own brain…), I had to ask "Where is this coming from?" The answer appeared obvious that they were being affected by someone from a more spiritual realm, something completely outside of themselves. As you read the following stories, you will agree that what people were being told they could not have known on their own.

Lu S., 46, Arizona, University News Bureau

A mother's horrifying dream shows her how to protect her son a full year before the circumstances occur.

"IN 1985, I HAD A MOST UNUSUAL DREAM that led to an extraordinary experience. In my dream, I was in a wilderness looking down at my 8 year-old son lying face down in wet sand a hundred feet below me at the base of a cliff. There was a chain across the top edge of the cliff and it was dark behind me and very bright and open in front of me. I could clearly see trees, bushes, rocks, and water which was not very deep as I looked down at the scene. This dream was so real that I was shaking as I woke up, and although relieved that it was not true, I was still troubled for a long time.

Approximately one year later, in October 1986, our family went with a group to the Grand Canyon to hike the Havasupai trail. My son Danny was nine years old at this point. We really were having a wonderful time when my husband suggested that we hike together to Mooney Falls. This was a fairly challenging feat, but we loved hiking and eagerly set off on this adventure with Danny being a typical nine-year-old racing ahead and skipping around on the rocks.

Suddenly I had an intense, urgent sense that he needed to be near us and so I called him back and sternly told him to stay right by us. I wasn't sure why this tremendously protective feeling came over me, but it was unbelievably powerful. As we emerged from the final tunnel, and I saw ahead a chain fence guarding the edge of the trail, a sickening twist in the pit of my stomach told me that the familiarity of this view came from the horrifying dream of the previous year.

I stared with mesmerized fascination at the scene around me: The tunnel behind us from which we had just emerged was the blackness that I remembered, the brightness ahead came from looking over the edge of the cliff at an empty expanse of sky. I sternly ordered Danny to stay back and gingerly crept to the edge, hanging onto the chain fence, as I stared down.

Just imagine my horror! There below was the exact tableau of my dream...the shallow stream, the rocks and bushes, the wet sand. The only missing element was the sad, broken body of an impetuous fun-loving child. Thank God my little boy was safe! I had the overwhelming sense that he had somehow escaped terrible harm.

It's almost as if he became sensitive to this when he assured me, "Don't worry Mom, I'll be really, really careful here today." He immediately became a cautious child, staying right between my husband and me holding us securely, never straying near the edge of the trail, stepping slowly and carefully along the path. We completed our hike safely and returned home a healthy, intact family, grateful forever for the protection of some unseen hand that guided our steps.

No one will ever convince me that what happened to me was some kind of coincidence; I am convinced that we were given a warning in time to choose to heed it and keep our family secure."

Sandy B., 43, Missouri, Health Care
Sandy's warning from her father changes vacation plans dramatically.

"IN 1992, I PLANNED A WONDERFUL SUMMER VACATION at a lake where I would share the expenses with another single parent who was a friend of mine. We were ecstatically looking forward to this when I had a very strange dream occur to me.

In the dream, my father, who had been dead for ten years, called me on the telephone and I was telling him excitedly about our upcoming adventure. My father replied very strongly, "Don't go!", but he wouldn't say why. When I awoke the next morning, the memory of this conversation was unusually strong, and it really disturbed me, so much so that I shared it with my friend. She agreed with me that it certainly was an odd dream.

The next night I had the same dream, only this time my father repeated his warning "Don't go!" even more insistently. I was so scared that I sat upright in bed and decided to call my friend to tell her that it had happened again. She was not thrilled...it was 4 a.m.

When we discussed it later that morning, I told her of my hesitance because of the intensity of his statement, and that I was really uncomfortable thinking about going on the trip. No matter how hard I tried to push down my anxious feelings, they repeatedly came back more strongly. I told my friend that I really thought I shouldn't go, but I felt very guilty for letting her down, and was tempted not to listen to the disruptive warning. My friend said, "I'm not mad" but I wasn't sure I totally believed her.

As our departure day arrived, my friend indeed did leave as scheduled and I felt torn between fluctuating feelings of guilt that I had deserted my friend, mild embarrassment that I was a worry wart, a kind of calm relief that I had made a decision and stuck with it, and disappointment that the lovely trip I had planned for and waited so long for had been destroyed and my vacation was a bust.

Imagine my horror at what happened next. On the way to the lake, my friend and her children were in a collision with a truck that crossed into their lane and caused an accident. My friend's five-year old son was killed, and her three-year old daughter was severely injured but survived. The child in the back seat died, and I sincerely believe that if we had gone on the vacation, my son would have been dead also because the two boys would have been together on that seat. It was a very long time before my friend and I could discuss this situation even though I was right beside her all through the funeral and hospital visits etc. We both had such intense emotion about this that it was a sensitive topic. I believe that my father was protecting his grandson from harm and I have always been so very grateful for that."

Yolanda (Yolie) C., 46, Arizona, Newspaper Editor
A mysterious dream gives Yolie the information to help her widowed aunt retrieve a large sum of money.

YOLIE EXPERIENCED AN UNUSUAL VISITATION that helped her aunt claim money owed to the family, and it couldn't have occurred without the help of her deceased uncle. "My uncle died of a heart attack, which was quite a shock to us because we had thought he was getting better in the hospital. His wife had not even made it back in time to be there with him when he passed away. It was a very heartrending thing for all the family to go through and my aunt and my mother were both devastated.

About a week after he died, I had a very strange dream. My uncle came to the door of our house and spoke to me. He was dressed in a kind of '50s style: cream-colored pants with cuffs, a white shirt with rolled-up sleeves, and I was startled to see him as a slender man when he was always a large person in life.

In my dream, I opened the door and he came into the house. He said to me, "I don't have much time, but I want to tell you two things: one, I don't want your mother, my sister, to cry for me because I am very happy. Two, go to see this woman (he gave me a name) at the Bureau of Reclamation because I have some money coming to me that your aunt can use."

I told my mother about this and she was anxious for me to give the details to my aunt (the widow). We did so; my aunt followed up on the information, and lo and behold! there was a $12,000 vested life insurance policy that she was unaware of. It was very helpful to the family."

Janice L., 46, Minnesota
Jan learns of her friend's gift in a dream.

"MY BEST FRIEND, JUDY, and her boyfriend were accidentally asphyxiated by carbon monoxide when they fell asleep in a car that was running. About a month afterward, my friend appeared to me in a dream and said, "I'm fine, don't worry about me because Blair and I are together and we're happy. I got you these two Rod McKuen albums for Christmas (she named two titles I was not familiar with) and I want you to have them."

When I woke up, I remembered the dream and the two albums she had mentioned, so I wrote down the names. Not long afterward, I was talking with Judy's mother and I asked if she had happened to see two record albums by Rod McKuen among Judy's things because she had mentioned purchasing them for me. I gave her the titles I had dreamed about. Her mother didn't seem to know anything about the records but said she would keep an eye out for them.

In my Christmas box from Judy's Mom was an unexpected gift... the two albums that Judy had told me about in the dream. A note was with them explaining that they had been in a bedroom drawer marked with "Jan" and everyone assumed they were for Judy's sister who was also named Jan. It was only when the mother took a closer look at what was there and found out that her daughter Jan didn't even like Rod McKuen that they put things together, realizing this was Judy's Christmas gift for me.

Because the information about the record albums was offered in the same dream where Judy told me she was O.K., I believed that I really had had some kind of contact with her and had not just imagined the whole thing."

Frances O., 39, Arizona, Parks and Recreation
Did Frances really run through the house to speak with her dead mother, or was it just a dream?

IN 1982, FRANCES'S MOTHER SUFFERED a very unexpected heart attack at 66, and the family was grieving terribly. Approximately one month after her mother's passing, Frances was awakened one night from a sound sleep by the sound of a ringing telephone. She jumped out of bed, and had to go through her own bedroom as well as a second bedroom to get to the living room.

"Because I was rushing, I stubbed my toe on the bed in the other bedroom and it hurt tremendously, but I kept going because I wanted to get to that telephone. When I answered I was shocked to hear my mother's voice speaking to me saying, "I don't want you to worry. I'm fine; everything is good here and I'm O.K." I responded, "Thank you, Momma, I love you." When I hung up, I felt very comforted and peaceful.

The next morning when I woke up, I remembered the unusual dream I had and wanted to call my sisters Jenny and Lisa to tell them about it. I didn't think it had really happened; I just thought it was a strange but comforting dream. As I stepped out of bed, my toe was in terrible pain, swollen and throbbing and when I went to the doctor later, I discovered that it was broken. Now my toe had been fine when I had gone to bed the previous evening.

With a shock, I realized that if my toe was injured, then I really had run to the other room to answer a telephone, and if I had really answered a phone, then I must have really spoken to my mother. Then it mustn't have been a dream after all!

While I don't have a logical explanation for how my dream might have happened, I do believe that my mother was happy and comfortable, and our whole family was strengthened and comforted by this knowledge. It made us feel very special to think that God would allow us to have such a unique experience."

Patricia Pahdongkei ("Looking at the Sun") B., 52, Oklahoma, Indian Health Service employee
Pahdongkei's dream prepares her to hear of her father's accident.

AS A FOUR-FOURTHS (FULL-BLOODED) Kiowa Indian married to a Comanche,

Pahdongkei has always been attuned to a more spiritual reality because the People typically focus in on the wisdom of the Spirit world more closely than the rest of us. It seemed very natural for her to receive messages in dreams and confer with elders about their meaning.

"In 1966, I had a dream in which I was walking down a hospital hallway. As I approached a patient's room, the man sat up in bed and looked at me although I could not seem to see his face. I had this same dream three nights in a row.

This concerned me greatly, so I went to my grandmother's house to ask her about the meaning of the dream. She told me to be ready to travel, and that she would pray about the meaning of the dream.

With that, I left her house, but decided to stop at the post office before going home. When I saw Louisa, the mail carrier, she said she thought there was something for me. When she looked closer, she told me instead that the telegram was for another family, but said that I was allowed to open it to check the information.

The telegram was from my sister! The message was indeed for me…my sister was telling me that my father had been seriously injured in an auto accident, and had been calling for me from his hospital bed. That certainly explained to me the meaning of my dream."

Barbara W., 33, California, Municipal Administration
A dream to prepare Barbara for a devastating event.

"MY FATHER WAS VERY ILL from a heart attack and was in critical condition when I prayed that I would give anything to have him pull through. I was pregnant at the time, and had a dream of a beautiful woman who told me that I should prepare for a devastating event in my life, and I should be strong and learn and no matter what happened I should not lose my faith. Of course, I automatically thought my father was going to die, but I was ecstatic when he didn't. However, the absolutely furthest thing from my mind occurred when my baby daughter died at birth.

This was a horribly negative time in my life, but interestingly enough I became more positive and peaceful and learned to appreciate life more. This awful event became a learning experience for me, and I now have two beautiful daughters."

LESSONS IN BELIEF

1. Because our dreams are so often fragmented, disoriented, and far-fetched, we often discount all information that comes to us in a dream as ridiculous. We must learn to be more attentive to those dreams that provide us relevant, valuable information.

2. For those who forget what a dream is about, paper and pencil near the bed are helpful to write down important details.

3. Others may not find us credible if we say, "This came to me in a dream" because of the general disdain society has for dreams. Our own strong belief in what we have learned is very important to carry our convictions through when others discount us.

4. The messages of dreams are very personal, and so our own intuitive interpretation is what is important. Others' interpretations may be interesting but are not paramount.

PERSONAL JOURNAL

Think about the following, and record any impressions:

1. Have I ever had a strange, unsettling, or unusual dream that did in fact offer me information that I needed to know?

2. What was the result of receiving the information my dream provided?

3. Did others have an opportunity to be aware of or react to my dream? What did they say or do?

4. In general, do I trust my dreams? What is my attitude toward them?

5. Do I need to more specifically record what is happening in my dreams?

INDIVIDUAL INSIGHTS OR OBSERVATIONS ABOUT "BELIEF" IN THE CIRCUMSTANCES OF MY LIFE:

Write in a journal any thoughts that come to mind.

Angels Are Companions in Near-Death Experiences

A Lesson in Peace

NOTHER TOPIC that I did not originally intend to discuss was what is referred to as the "near-death experience" because other books and articles have covered this topic exhaustively. Again, I found that so many people told me about truly unique things that had happened to them that I could not resist the chance to research this phenomenon first-hand. By capturing the examples that people shared with me where they had met deceased family members or other Beings of Light, whom they perceived as angels, I discovered some amazing stories. I think you'll find them as interesting as I did.

Julie A., 43, Utah, Housewife
A dying son cannot stay with his father because he is needed by the rest of the family.

"MY UNCLE HAD AN UNUSUAL near-death experience when he was hospitalized with life-threatening emphysema in 1988. It later served a marvelous healing purpose within our family. As he described it to us later, he left his body and was walking on a "rosy path" when he encountered his father sitting on a bench along the pathway.

His father spoke to him, "Come sit here with me for awhile." My uncle was overjoyed to see his father who had also died some time earlier from a severe and painful emphysema. He sat down gratefully saying, "How are you Dad? Are you in pain?" His father replied, "No, I am at peace and I am very happy." My uncle replied, "Then I am ready to be here with you and be peaceful and comfortable too." My grandfather said to him, "No, you musn't walk any further down this path. You're needed by your mother and ...(he mentioned several other family members). You need to go back to them."

At his urging, my uncle reluctantly left and walked back down the path the way he had come. He came back to consciousness and survived that bout with his illness but did not say anything right at that time about what he had experienced.

Several years later, at a family gathering when my grandmother and six of her kids (including the uncle I have been talking about) were sitting and reminiscing about family memories, the talk turned to how difficult it had been at the time of my grandfather's death. There was a lot of sorrow in the room about how painful it had been for him. My uncle spoke up and told about meeting his father when he had almost died from his emphysema and the talk they had sitting on that bench. He told of how comfortable, peaceful, and happy his father was, and that their grandfather had sent him back to be with the people in that room to let them know.

He had not spoken of it sooner because the family had not all been gathered in the same place. The feeling of joy and consolation that filled the room was just indescribable, and a wonderful healing occurred for all of the painful memories that had been held by those present."

Ed C., 49, Massachusetts, Psychologist
Near-death at a dinner party opens the door to another dimension.

"I WAS AT A DINNER PARTY at my parents' home when I was 18 years old that turned into a most memorable affair. I was not feeling sick in any way, but I began to feel my head sinking towards the table, and suddenly became unable to hear as I was surrounded with silence. My last thought before I lost consciousness was that my face was awfully close to the soup.

The next thing I knew, my body was lying on the floor beside my chair to the right where my mother had been sitting. My feet were toward the table and my head toward the wall of the dining room. I could see my mother and the other guests gathered around my feet, and my father, a doctor, was checking my mouth to see if I was choking. I seemed to be about five feet above them, suspended in mid-air, looking down at the scene.

I could *feel* my parents' worry, but could not hear their voices or any other sound. As I looked up, I could clearly see four small beings dressed in robes of a kind of white cloth. They had similar, pleasant expressions and spoke to me telepathically. They seemed to say not to worry, that I was safe and in the presence of love.

The beings invited me to look down toward the body lying on the floor, and told me that I had a choice, *which was mine to make.* I could stay with them, or go back to that body. I responded to them without sound and without moving my lips, and said that I did want to stay with them, but had important things to do, so I needed to return.

The moment I thought/said that, I experienced the most extraordinary feeling of total and blissful love, happiness, joy, and peace. It was the most wonderful thing I had ever felt in my entire life. I knew somehow that it was this that I was leaving, but that I would return to it someday, and for now had to complete a mission on earth. And so it was decided.

With that decision, I heard a "sucking" sound and felt myself being physically pulled back into my body with a hissing of air, and suddenly became intensely conscious of the *noise of earth*. It was so very different from the deep quiet and peaceful emptiness I had just left.

I convinced my parents I was alright and just needed some air, and went outside to reflect alone on what had happened to me. The awesomeness of this experience was beyond words and I did not share it with anyone for years. My parents had a whole battery of EEG tests done to guarantee that I had not had some kind of stroke, but there was no evidence (and to this day never has been) of any physical illness.

I finally told my parents about this more than twenty years after it occurred when my father was struck with terminal prostate cancer. They listened wide-eyed in amazement. I told my father that I wanted to share this with him because of what he was going through, and there was absolutely nothing to be afraid of: that he was headed for light and peace and there were beings and angels waiting for him. They were surprised that I had kept this to myself all these years, but I tried to explain that the experience was so far beyond what words can describe, that I didn't know how to express it.

I believe that my father received a truly genuine sense of inner peace and calm that stayed with him until his death, and I felt so privileged to have provided him that."

Paul C., 51, Arizona, Civil Engineer
A terrifying accident offers a teenager a choice…

"SIX YEARS AGO, my daughter was 13 years old and attended a YMCA camp for an enriching summer experience. They were riding horses one day and the instructors were mostly up in the stands, while the kids were in the arena with the horses when a horrifying thing happened.

My daughter walked behind a horse at the moment that a bee stung it, and she was kicked directly in the middle of her face and landed almost a quarter of the arena away. You could see the imprint of the horse's hoof in the center of her face. While she didn't have external cuts, everything in her entire face was broken except her chin. Her nose was even broken in seven places and she remained unconscious for 30 minutes.

The doctors told us later, "We do know how to deal with this type of trauma, but we haven't seen anyone live through it to be able to tell you exactly a pattern of recovery."

While she was unconscious, my daughter had the kind of thing people call a near-death experience where she moved toward a tremendous light in a state of warmth and peace, and was met by a comforting man who walked with her into some sort of library. He sat and talked serenely with her about how she had much work to do in her life, and she had a choice to stay where it was peaceful or to go back, but it was her decision. She chose to go back.

Today she still is working on a lot of things like improving memory retention, but basically she is doing quite well. Her experience has given her a burning desire to work with people and serve them so she hopes to go into the medical field. With her determination to succeed, we think she'll make it."

Steve C., 41, Arizona, Building Services/School District
Steve's near-drowning causes a most unusual experience.

WHEN HE WAS IN HIGH SCHOOL, Steve and a group of friends ditched school one time and decided to go hang out at the Verde River. They saw some acquaintances on the other side, and decided to swim across because the river looked fairly calm. That was deceptive! The surface may have seemed unruffled, but the currents underneath were very strong. Steve tired as fought the vicious stream, and gradually realized that he wasn't going to be able to make it across. As he struggled to get closer to shore, he was being swept back into the center.

"When I got near one of my friends, I tried to grab David's leg, even scratched him severely in the process, but in the end, I was helplessly swept away. I remember floating on my back and seeing the sky and I must have gone underwater because suddenly the sky looked different…dreamy and faraway. I was experiencing new feelings too. Where I had been chilled badly, suddenly I felt no coldness whatsoever. I had been terrified and panicked, and then I was completely calm and happy; I felt as if I had no worries. Also I remember absolute silence; I did not hear any sound at all.

Almost in slow motion I began to see scenes from my early childhood which were incredibly detailed. I saw houses and rooms and people that I don't really consciously remember except for that "movie-like" trance. This seemed to go on for a very long time. I now believe that I was very near death, probably from drowning.

Suddenly my head struck a branch of a tree that extended into the water, and I abruptly roused from my dreamlike state and grabbed it. My friends who had been chasing me down the bank of the river (I was totally unaware of them) climbed down and rescued me. I hadn't died!

I left the river almost immediately since I was in such a weak state. When I got home, I told my mother what had happened to me, and while she was mildly doubtful, she did confirm that the details I was relating about houses and people were all true. What was odd was that she told me that I had been to those homes of friends and relatives when I was only a year or two old and I was so young that it didn't seem possible that I would remember them.

At this point, I believe that I was near death and was in some kind of state where parts of my life were reviewed, or where my brain was accessing different information than when in a conscious, normal mode. It would have been very easy to just "slip over" to the other side from where I was in that place of dreamy peace. I think it was a small miracle that I lived!"

One other time, Steve found himself very fortuitously removed from a harmful situation when his friends piled into a station wagon and decided to drive out-of-town for a party. They wanted Steve to go with them, but he felt so oddly uncomfortable about it that he chose to go and take his history test instead. Now, that was very unlike Steve! They *really* razzed him about that, and left without him.

"The car hit a bad bump just before a bridge, and the driver lost control causing the car to roll many times. About 6-8 kids were in the station wagon, and it was incredibly lucky that no one was killed, although there were a lot of very severe injuries. I didn't even find out about the accident until the mother of one of my friends called to see how I was, thinking that I had been hurt too since I went everywhere the group went. To this day, I don't know what it was that prompted me so strongly not to go in the car, but someone very definitely was looking out for my safety, and it could very well have been a guardian angel."

Kathleen K., 41, Arizona, Professional Psychic
Kathleen's brother has a strange experience at an accident scene.

KATHLEEN RELATES A STORY about her brother who was driving an 18-wheeler diesel truck that slid on a treacherous patch of ice and water on a freeway and crashed. The truck was demolished and her brother reports leaving his body and observing people coming to his aid.

"My brother could feel himself floating outside of his truck and looking down on the scene from above where his immobile body was clearly visible. As he re-entered his body and "came to", he surprised all of the people who were at the accident by simply getting up and walking away unharmed. No one who looked at the damaged truck could believe that someone involved in that wreck could escape without injury."

Rita E., 44, Iowa, Agricultural Sales

Rita's constant companion helps pull her through after a terrible accident.

"I WAS ONCE INVOLVED in a fatal car accident in which my two children, three years old and six months old, were both killed. My own injuries were life-threatening...collapsed lung, broken ribs, bruised heart, and internal bleeding.

Immediately after the accident, I remember a very calm, comforting voice, which seemed male, that spoke to me continuously saying things like, "Keep breathing, close your eyes and concentrate on yourself and your breathing, everything will be taken care of..."

Now, you need to understand that this was not the voice of any human being at the scene of the accident, but some kind of otherworldly voice. How do I know that, you may wonder? Because that voice was with me as I drifted in and out of consciousness for the next week. That voice was speaking to me when nobody else was in the room, and it was the same calm, gentle tones that I had heard right from the beginning. That presence was with me all the time I was in the I.C.U.

What is even more remarkable is that after I recovered, I went on to have two more children despite being told that I would never have any because my husband had been affected by chemicals. The experiences I have related here convinced me that there is some kind of special help and guidance offered to us that we may not always understand or deserve, but I guess we just have to be thankful for."

Faith A., 30, Iowa, Hospital Computer Department
Faith meets her son...before his birth!

"WHEN I WAS IN LABOR WITH MY SON, I went into a "code blue" which generated a lot of activity and commotion among the staff members. As this occurred, I drifted up above everyone in the room, and sort of looked down upon the scene with mild curiosity. I think I realized somehow that I was the one responsible for all the fuss, but didn't feel particularly worried about it.

In fact, I watched with increasing fascination as Father performed the last rites of the Church on this person who looked like me, but all I could feel was a kind of relaxed contentment.

Suddenly, I realized I was not watching this alone. I knew that my not-yet-born son was watching everything with me. Until this point, I had not yet known the gender of the baby I had been carrying, but here he was, a very wise-seeming creature. What a way to meet!

My son was somehow communicating with me, and the message that was very clear was, "You'll be fine and everything will turn out alright." How odd it was to have this wordless conversation in a place that seemed to have no walls, floors, ceilings, or confinement.

All of a sudden, it felt like I simply drifted off to sleep, and when I awoke, I was alive and so was my new baby...a son. Why was I not surprised? Today my little boy is three years old and we have the most incredibly special bond. It may have originated during the eight days we had to spend in the I.C.U. together immediately after the birth, or, as I recalled what I had experienced during labor, that bond may have started pre-birth in some place I had never been to before."

Kim S., 33, California, Publishing Company
Kim has unusual encounters after a major accident.

"FOLLOWING A LIFE-THREATENING CAR ACCIDENT, I was in a coma for four days, drifting in a wonderful, calm place. Apparently, I had sustained serious nerve damage, and although I could periodically hear those around me, I could not respond to them in any way.

I had some unusual experiences while in this non-responsive state as I encountered the spiritual forms of people I had known and loved in my childhood. They told me that I was "on the edge", and I seemed to understand that this was a place of choice where I might go in either direction.

There seemed to be a message such as "Get rid of all the obstacles..." At some point after that, I regained consciousness with a sense that the choice had been made. Although I recovered, I have some strange "after effects" that the doctors cannot explain...I de-magnetize watches and credit cards etc.

I have also spoken to other people who have gone through a near-death experience, and they have a similar tale; we are typically unable to wear watches because they stop altogether, or run faster or slower than normal."

Pat C., 52, Illinois, Medical Management
An allergic reaction to medicine sends Bob toward a bright light.

"WHEN MY SON, BOB, came home from college one year, we were having a pleasant breakfast when he suddenly began having severe chest pain. He is an asthmatic, so we immediately think "lungs" rather than "heart attack." When I called the doctor, I was told to have Bob take his pleurisy medicine which would have been a normal procedure.

However, this time was different. My son had an extreme allergic reaction to the medicine and told me that he needed to get to the hospital without delay. Things rapidly got worse. In the car, he turned purple and when they tried to put him in a wheelchair at the emergency room, his legs were already getting stiff. He was no longer responding, so they used the paddles to shock him.

At that point Bob technically was dead. When he came back later, the experience he described was as follows: he traveled toward a bright light, and saw hands that he understood were friendly, supportive, and meant to help him; but he didn't know to whom they belonged. He felt tremendously peaceful, knew that he was in a beautiful place and was aware that he wanted to tell me that he loved me but he couldn't. Apparently, he was experiencing a strong yearning to come back and communicate with me, and as that grew, he found the bright light fading, the hands disappeared, and he came back to life.

At the time that Bob told us about what had happened to him, it was years ago and no one had yet written about what we now call "near-death" experiences. Today, what he described has been written about frequently, and is quite consistent with the other events that people recount, so we are certain that what happened to him was real.

I have always been a little more sensitive to spiritual messages because of something that happened to me as a teenager. I was driving away from my home, and had only gone maybe a mile, when an internal voice told me to go back. I was kind of surprised, but did pay attention, and was told to go to my grandmother's which was just one house away from ours.

When I arrived, I discovered that my grandmother had just had a stroke, and I was able to get help for her. Although she did pass away much later, this time I was able to help her in time. Those little voices inside, I believe, are a real source of inspiration."

Ida R., 61, Colorado, Custom Home Development
A man encountered during surgery offers words of comfort.

"IN SEPTEMBER 1980, I had open heart surgery for mitral valve repair, and during the surgery while I was under the anesthetic, a very strange thing happened. I saw a white form at the foot of my bed and it spoke to me. This was a man with white hair and white clothing, and he seemed friendly and comforting. The message he gave me was "You'll be alright now."

My partner in the hospital room told me that my doctor said I had almost died at one point during the surgery, and that must have been when my friend appeared. I have always been a believer in the action of God in our lives, and the presence of angels, and I feel very grateful for the experience I had because I know for certain that someone is taking care of me."

Chris Y., 46, California, Fast Food Industry
A skateboard accident leads a young man to an unusual experience.

"WHEN MY SON WAS JUST 18 YEARS OLD, he had a terrible skateboard accident. As kids that age will do, he was engaged in a very risky venture—being towed by a car as he hung on for a faster ride. When he fell off the skateboard, because of the speed the car was moving, he sustained a massive head injury and lost consciousness at the scene.

As he described to us later, my son was "up above himself" as paramedics lifted him into an ambulance on a backboard, and he saw a very bright light while he was feeling warm and very calm. Although he has never spoken to me of encountering any beings during this experience, to this day he has no fear of death or fear of God, and the faith of every family member has been increased because of this incident. My son successfully went through brain surgery needed for a blood clot, and has completely recovered to our great relief."

LESSONS IN PEACE

1. So often, people fear death, but those who have been there describe an overwhelming, almost incomprehensible peace. The lesson for the rest of us is that we do not need to dread a reality that every human being will undergo, but can approach it with a sense of reassurance.

2. At a moment of great stress where we are poised somewhere between life and death, we must surrender to the great light and know that we will be led.

3. For many who encounter spiritual beings and are given a choice about staying or returning, if they return to an earthly plane, their lives are forever changed because they do not fear the moment when they will go back to that place of great peace forever.

PERSONAL JOURNAL

Think about the following, and record any impressions:

1. Have I ever personally been close to death? What sensations did I feel, what people did I see, what did I hear, and what actions occurred?

2. Have I ever thought about my own death? What feelings have emerged when I did so?

INDIVIDUAL INSIGHTS OR OBSERVATIONS ABOUT "PEACE" IN THE CIRCUMSTANCES OF MY LIFE:

Write in a journal any thoughts that come to mind.

Angels Are Friends in Wartime

A Lesson in Responsibility

FEW OF THE PEOPLE I interviewed had experienced quite unusual things during a war, so I created a special place to record them in this chapter. The men and women who are called to serve their country are offering the greatest sacrifice that any human being can—to put their own lives in jeopardy for the benefit of others. When I heard the examples below, I could only believe that because of the enormity of this responsibility, the angels must take special care of the people who are serving. The stories that I heard personally are just a few of the thousands that must exist out there.

Robert Luikens, 71, Arizona, Retired salesperson, Military Intelligence Specialist WWII

A soldier miraculously escapes several bombs.

WHILE OTHER PEOPLE WRITTEN about in this book are identified only by their first name, readers need to know that this man is special because he is my father, and he died just three months after relating these extraordinary experiences to me.

I had heard only scattered details of his wartime adventures throughout my growing-up years, as well as when I was an adult. Although he did not always speak of his personal experiences to his children, my Dad had built a considerable library of excellent historical books on war and was somewhat of an expert on tactics and strategies. However, when I told him about my mission of speaking with people regarding truly miraculous encounters during their lives, he chose to tell me something that he had never before even hinted at: that he felt his life had been spared in an unexplained way on several occasions during World War II. He felt that there must have been some special reason why he escaped death when there was no rational way to explain it away as being "just plain lucky." This is exactly what he described to me:

"In England, the "buzz bombs" (V-I rockets) had just started coming across the English channel around June 12, 1944...about 10 days after the invasion of Normandy. The Germans were frantically trying to get the V-2 bomb sites ready for Allied attacks, and on June 16 the bombs were coming very heavily.

I was at Woodchurch working in an isolated intelligence trailer that night because the next day's operations orders always came in during the night in code to a communications trailer, and someone had to go over and pick them up to bring back to the intelligence area. We would then prepare briefings to get all planes, troops, and arms ready for movement first thing in the morning.

On this night at Woodchurch, approximately 2:30 a.m., as I walked from trailer to trailer near the pierced plank temporary runway (sheets of metal laid down by engineers), a huge British anti-aircraft battery began blasting away at the buzz bombs overhead. Although we were on a direct line between London and the French coast, we didn't typically worry that the bombs would fall on us because they were aimed further inland.

It was unfortunate timing that the anti-aircraft began firing at the very moment I was unprotected, because one of the shells did not explode at 2,000 feet where it was supposed to, and I knew that shell was coming back down when I heard the whining sound. Only a few hundred feet above me it exploded with the most deafening boom I have ever heard.

The shrapnel landed on the metal runway with a noisy clattering like a hailstorm, and the explosion tore up and shattered an enormous old tree that had stood near the runway like a sentinel welcoming back our pilots. Huge branches and other large pieces of wood were flung like matchsticks in every direction, and I was lying flat on my face in the midst of this praying that I would make it through.

As the racket diminished, my captain shouted from the door of the intelligence trailer, asking if I was alright. "I don't know, I'm afraid to move...", I hollered back, relieved to hear the sound of my own voice although my ears still rang from the blast and my eyes seemed blinded.

Slowly, I stood up and walked in a daze to the doorway where the captain waited. He was astounded to see that I didn't have a scratch or mark on me anywhere, and declared that it was surely a miracle. We didn't discover how much of a miracle it really was until daylight when we could survey the damage to the area, and saw the massive amounts of rubble from the remains of the tree, runway, and shrapnel.

The only completely clear spot for a radius of hundreds of yards was a tiny depression in the earth just the size of my body where I had been desperately praying for help and must have been covered by an angel's wing. The idea that I was just lucky doesn't seem terribly plausible as I remember the incredible destruction I witnessed, and realized that something very special had happened."

*   *   *

"I had several other close calls shortly after that when we went to France as part of an advance party. One of the most vivid in my mind was the time I was alone in the communications hut when a seriously crippled P-47 was trying to land with an armed "hung bomb." The 500 lb. bomb had released from its forward hook during the mission but was still attached to the back one. In this kind of situation, the pilot was usually killed upon landing as the bomb and plane both exploded.

Someone had telephoned to tell me "Bob, get out of that hut as fast as you can; you're in the path of a hung bomb." But it was too late! As I listened, I looked out the window and saw that the plane was only about 200 feet away and landing at that very moment. Vibration from the runway planking jarred the bomb loose and as I watched transfixed, the bomb hurtled end-over-end right in front of me past the window before coming to a silent stop.

I couldn't believe it. The bomb was a dud! Our percentage of duds at that time was very low—maybe 1%—since we were producing extremely high quality weaponry. 99 out of 100 times, that bomb would have exploded on the runway, killing both the pilot and me, and destroying the plane and the hut.

A second time we weren't so fortunate. A badly wounded pilot couldn't control his plane as he was trying to land, his wing tip vertical to the ground so that he was literally flying at a 90 degree angle. As he tried frantically to level his plane, the wing tip hit the ground and spun the plane out of control right past our building into the woods where it crashed with a fiery explosion. Sadly, he was killed. Except for some extraordinary protective influence, he would have hit our building as he careened past unable to maneuver the plane. "

* * *

A final story reflects the angel's ability to offer a split-second warning in time to avert disaster.

"Four of us were traveling in the dead of night returning from Friedrichshafen (the German zeppelin base) after investigating the area for what became an aborted troop move. It turned out that the orders had been superseded even as we were preparing the move.

Near the town of Ulm, the driver wanted to take a shortcut to avoid the populated areas and although he had a map, we almost went into the Danube River. We did not know that the bridge had been destroyed, but as we sped down the pitch dark, narrow, rutted road, I suddenly had an uncomfortable feeling and shouted for the driver to stop. He brought the jeep to a skidding, shuddering halt seemingly an inch from the edge of a cliff! The bridge marked on that map was gone...bombed out.

The walls of the bluff were so steep at that point that they looked like a canyon, and as we all climbed shakily out of the vehicle and walked gingerly to the edge, the only thing we could see was a faint, shining ribbon far below where some light gleamed on the water's surface. We were probably a couple of hundred feet above the river. Our hearts were beating wildly as we realized how close we had come to sailing right over the edge. The only thing that stopped us was that eerie silent warning, a feeling that something wasn't quite as it should be.

Some of the things we did seem very strange now. Quite a few of us were standing around one time watching incoming rounds of 20 mm cannon shells, and as I moved abruptly, a shell landed at the exact place where I had been standing. Don't ask me now why we were watching those shells... Actually, I can't explain any reason why I should have been so blessed as to escape not just once, but several times, from what would have been a sure death.

I like to think that my life has made a contribution and that the children I had are also giving something back to the world, and that may be the reason why I received special protection. Whatever it may have been, I'm grateful."

Lloyd G., 50, Arizona, Shop Supervisor
Lloyd awakens a fraction of a second before a bayonet is buried in his neck.

"WHEN I WAS ON A PERIMETER GUARD duty in Vietnam, I had a most incredible experience. I was in a two-man foxhole where we alternated sleeping and watching. I had finished my watch at approximately 2 a.m., awakened my partner, and settled down for a good rest with my rifle behind me as our procedures required.

I found out later that I had been asleep for approximately 20 minutes only, when *I felt something grab me and shake me awake.* This should have been the time when I was sleeping most heavily. An enemy soldier stood over me with the point of a bayonet buried about one inch into my neck; he was ready to slit my throat.

At this point he was only about two feet away from me, and my partner was already dead from his knife. I had no choice but to kill him to protect myself even though I am not happy that I had to do it.

My impression was that someone was shaking me and alerting me; whether you can call this "being" an angel I don't know, but I am convinced that something extraordinary occurred. I didn't awaken accidentally, and my partner who was dead could not have helped me in any way. I feel that I was specifically saved in order to accomplish something in this life, so I feel a responsibility to make a contribution.

I feel that the fact that I was even in the military in the first place was a kind of small miracle. When I was a junior in high school, I was a passenger in a car that was involved in a serious accident. I was paralyzed for six weeks, and blind for about six months from a severe hematoma. As that was relieved, I began to see more and more clearly, and ultimately recovered well enough that I could pass a Marine Corps entrance physical two years later.

To have survived such a terrible accident only to have my throat slit in a foxhole seems incongruous, so the only conclusion I can come to is that this is part of a larger plan. I even had one further experience after the war that reinforced the sense of purpose. My ex-wife and I were traveling on a dirt road when a large anthill at the side gave way as we passed and the road disappeared from under us. Our truck literally fell off the side of the roadway.

This was a potentially life-threatening situation for us because we had heard of a man a few months earlier who had an identical set of circumstances, and his truck had rolled five or six times down an embankment decapitating him.

As our truck fell off the roadway at an angle, and began to tip, it came to rest against a very delicate jojoba bush and stopped long enough for us to crawl out and escape unharmed. As we looked at the fragile bush holding the truck, we were astounded that the vehicle hadn't just crushed the tiny branches as it rolled over them. There was no logical reason that the truck should have stopped but we saw it happen.

Again, I had an overwhelming sense of being saved for a very special reason. I have dedicated my life to making a difference on this planet, and I am now perfectly willing to believe in the presence of beings who help humans make that happen."

Lloyd is a gentle-appearing person and somewhat soft-spoken, who is sincere in his conviction that he has been saved from fatal events. One of the most striking testimonies as you speak with him is the one-inch white scar on the left side of his neck that bears mute witness to the terror of awakening to an enemy soldier holding a knife that is penetrating your skin.

Ilia L., Texas, Military Personnel
A miraculous escape from a land mine happens for this young woman.

ILIA IS NOT ASHAMED TO SPEAK to you about her special angel whom she calls Paul. She believes that he is an important protector and took exceptional care of her during the Gulf War. An incident occurred during the conflict where she accidentally drove over a mine outside of Bosra in Iraq. To her amazement, Ilia was untouched by the shrapnel which flew over her and landed all around her destroying machinery and equipment, but leaving her miraculously safe in the middle of the debris. She is convinced that her life was spared for a reason.

LESSONS IN RESPONSIBILITY

1. Those who are responsible for the safety and protection of others may indeed be protected in a very special way themselves in order to carry out their responsibilities.

2. In times of extraordinary stress and pressure, we should look for extraordinary examples of shielding from harm.

PERSONAL JOURNAL

Think about the following, and record any impressions:

1. Have I ever felt that I was being taken care of in order to perform some task or mission that I was responsible for?

INDIVIDUAL INSIGHTS OR OBSERVATIONS ABOUT "RESPONSIBILITY" IN THE CIRCUMSTANCES OF MY LIFE:

Write in a journal any thoughts that come to mind.

Angels Support Only If
We Allow Them

A Lesson in Surrender

HIS CHAPTER WILL EXPLORE the consequences of ignoring the warnings and leadings that we are blessed with. The people you will meet in the following stories did, in fact, receive the offering of an angel hand and chose to ignore it. The lesson that many of these individuals learned is that the voice they hear and the feelings they feel are so faint and slight that to disregard them as irrelevant or meaningless can have dire results.

Even if the warning is strong, we may still choose to ignore it since we have our own will and are allowed to make our own choices. Each of the people you will read about below could have made different choices but were affected in some way by the consequences of their actions.

Ronnie M., 39, California, Speaker/Trainer
A sense of dread accompanies Ronnie to Florida.

IN APRIL 1990, Ronnie was preparing for a speaking tour in Florida, and for several days before her departure she was filled with a sense of dread. In fact, as the trip came closer she became almost physically ill thinking about getting on the plane. Now Ronnie had been doing this type of work for some time, so it was a very ordinary type of trip for her to take.

"The night before I was scheduled to leave, I became so agitated that I just couldn't sleep. As I was lying in bed, I saw a presence in my room that seemed to have on a flowing white garment, a rather androgynous figure that said to me, "Don't go!" I also seemed to feel a physical touch from this figure at the same time.

The next morning I felt very nervous when I got up, and I called my client and asked if I could be relieved of this assignment and could they send someone else? Unfortunately, they were unwilling to do this and insisted that I go to Florida anyway since there was no time to find a replacement. I got on the plane with a feeling of intense dread, and my stomach was so unsettled that I became physically sick as we got closer to Florida. I had made hundreds of business trips, but never before had I experienced feelings such as these. I was both puzzled and scared at the same time.

I had arrived in Florida one day early to relax before my speaking assignments, and within 24 hours, even before my first program, my rental car was hit by a truck. I was thrown out on the concrete on my head, suffered severe injuries, and my time in Florida ended up being spent in a hospital in Intensive Care. It took me approximately six months to return to health after this accident and I had major complications. One serious result of the trauma was a problem called "dysnomia" where I could describe the function of something I was looking at but did not know what it was called. I could tell you what a fork was used for but would call it a spoon.

What I learned from this is that I have to be very sensitive to any feelings or thoughts that I have, and pay attention to the information I am given."

Norma T., 35, Texas, Language Training
A busy train station sets the stage for disaster.

NORMA WAS IN ZURICH on a business trip standing and looking at the hotel information board when a hurried but intense thought passed through her mind: "Norma, get your wallet, bring it closer to you!" Her purse was with her luggage behind her, but she hesitated because her attention was being distracted, and before she turned to retrieve her purse, it had been stolen! Norma's main worry was about her passport rather than her cash, and so she prayed that somehow she would be able to straighten everything out.

"I decided to call the American Embassy to see what procedures I might have to put in place, and just over an hour later I received a call to come in person to the Embassy office. I discovered that a Swiss mail service employee had found my passport in a mailbox and had taken the time to bring it to the Embassy, something that they assured me *had never been done before!* All of the clerks were coming over to see who was this lucky person who had recovered her passport. They told me that numerous thefts occur every year to travelers, but that no one had been fortunate enough to recover a stolen passport. I know *someone* must have been taking care of me!"

Lu S., 46, Arizona, University News Bureau
A violent husband endangers the friend of his wife.

LU TELLS OF AN OCCASION where she was being sent specific warning messages and chose to ignore them, producing potentially serious consequences. In 1981, she had met a girlfriend for a workout at a health club. The friend was married, although staying in a badly abusive relationship, while Lu was single at the time following a divorce.

She and her friend decided to go out to eat afterward, and were enjoying the comfortable conversation so much that time passed faster than they realized, and it got quite late. Several times, a small voice inside her head had said, "You really need to leave." Even though the tiny voice became quite insistent, Lu didn't really make any effort to take her friend home and they continued to enjoy their evening.

Finally, they realized that it was very late, and left the restaurant. Without any conscious thought about why she was doing it, she locked her door and rolled up the window despite the oppressively hot night and lack of air conditioning in the vehicle. Lu could not, at the time, understand the feeling of dread and anxiety that overwhelmed her as they approached her friend's house, but it built steadily.

As they pulled into her friend's driveway, the husband came running out of the house up to the car and tried to pull the door open on the driver's side where she was sitting, but could not because she had uncharacteristically locked it. He pounded on the window, but didn't make any progress there either because it was rolled up. Lu uttered a silent prayer of thanks that something had made her close things tight since she rarely, if ever, drove with doors and windows secured.

The friend's husband, now in a violent rage, suddenly bent over out of sight beside the car for a minute and then just as abruptly reappeared with a large rock in his hand with which he began to pound upon the window trying to break it. Lu's friend (the man's wife) jumped from the vehicle on the passenger side, screamed at her to get away, and ran into the house.

Lu did safely escape the driveway, and found out later that the jealous husband thought she was a man keeping his wife out late. If the window had been rolled down, or the driver's door unlocked, and he had been able to strike Lu with the rock, she would have been badly injured or worse before he discovered his mistake.

Lu states, "If I had only not ignored the voice that was telling me to leave the restaurant, this would never have happened. If I had taken my friend home at the normal time, we would not have encountered her husband because he would have been at work. One very strange thing is that the next time I was in my friend's driveway, I noticed that the area where he picked up the rock was entirely grass, and I have always wondered where that rock came from that he tried to attack me with. The lesson I learned is that I will certainly listen better to the internal voices next time."

Raylene B., 29, Arizona, Health Care
Raylene receives a distinctly bad feeling about having her visitors leave the house.

"WE HAD FRIENDS VISITING who had brought their five-year old child with them, and we were having a really good time. When they mentioned that it was time to go, I started having a particularly bad feeling, but I couldn't identify specifically what it was. I suggested that they stay but they seemed to want to get on their way. As the feeling grew stronger, I urged them more seriously, "I really do wish you wouldn't go." That funny feeling was getting worse and worse.

Our friends did leave anyway, and about 5-10 minutes later we heard sirens nearby, and I said in horror, "That's Pat and Jackie, I just know it!" I had never been so certain of anything. I wanted to go out looking for them, but my family said that without knowing which way they had gone, that was a silly thing to do. And so I waited for a phone call that I was certain was coming.

Sure enough! The phone rang and it was our friends who were at the hospital. Their baby had been injured in the accident and the hospital staff wanted to keep the child overnight for observation. Our friends wanted to return to spend the night with us while they waited for word."

Mamie J., 35, Michigan, Driver for Airport Transportation Company
A vacation interferes with a chance to see a good friend for the last time.

MAMIE WORKS HARD, spending long hours behind the wheel of a van for a transportation company, ferrying visitors back and forth from the airport to other destinations. If she has a chance for leisure time, it is a precious luxury to her, and when some friends asked her to accompany them on a trip it meant a good opportunity for her to get away.

Even as Mamie looked forward to the trip, she was getting a pretty strong message that she shouldn't go, and no matter how hard she tried to ignore it, a little voice was telling her to stay home.

"I really should have paid attention to that voice, because it was bad for me to go on that trip. I didn't have that good of a time, and spent money I shouldn't have spent so then I couldn't pay some of my bills that were due when I came back. But the worst thing of all was that I had talked about seeing a very good friend during the same time I was away on the trip, and because I was gone I didn't get to see her.

It was a terrible thing…10 days after I got back, she died from a massive blood clot to the lungs and so did her four-month old baby that would have been my godchild. I have felt so guilty ever since (the death had occurred about six weeks prior to the time Mamie was relating this story) and I keep wishing I had listened to the voice that was talking to me, instead of being pigheaded and doing whatever I wanted to do."

Mamie's story is so typical of human desire to get our needs fulfilled, by doing things against our better judgment that ultimately do not work for our good. The kind of experience she relates is a powerful but painful lesson that may result in a more attentive listening the next time a small voice tries to guide.

Trisha E., 37, Michigan, Dental Receptionist
While Trisha is at the hair salon, her house is burning.

A VIBRANT PERSON who sparkles with energy, Trisha turned serious as she told a story about a Thanksgiving in Maryland in 1990 that the family will never forget. As she was driving home from work two days before Thanksgiving and headed toward a hair appointment, she heard a voice that said "Go home! Go home! Go home!" She looked at the clock in her car and thought, "Surely everything will be alright until I get back from the salon. These appointments are almost impossible to get."

Although she felt a little apprehensive, she continued to the beauty shop and had her hair done, returning home immediately after she was finished, assuring herself all the way that everything would be O.K.

She was wrong! As she pulled into her street, it was lined with emergency vehicles. Trisha discovered that while she was gone, her house had burned, and in fact was on fire at the precise time she had looked at the clock in her car in response to the insistent inner voice.

"What I could be really grateful about in the midst of the horror at losing our house was that my son was able to get out safely and was not hurt. We did have our family together and safe that year for Thanksgiving so we were able to be thankful after all."

David B., 24, Arizona, Computer Systems Administration
David ignores a warning, causing an accident.

"I HAD AN ACCIDENT that I think now could have been prevented if I had paid closer attention to a little voice inside. Someone had broken into my car and stole a cassette deck, cracking the one-piece dashboard in the process. I had worked hard to get everything replaced (and spent about $500) on the stereo, dash, and components.

It was almost time to leave for my college class, but I wanted to do a quick test run first to make sure there were no rattles or electrical problems and that everything was working. I was driving east past a major intersection, when a thought popped into my head…"If I'm not careful, I'll have an accident."

Of course, I immediately let that thought escape from my head. I drove about a mile farther and decided to turn around and go back the way I had come so I could head on to class. At the very intersection I had passed a few moments before and where I had been given a cautionary thought, I had an accident.

It was my fault; I thought the light was green, and ran a red light, hitting a truck that was going through the intersection correctly. It wasn't just the two of us involved—the spare tire on the back of the truck swung around and demolished the rear end of a passing Cadillac. They were not happy people…

The lesson I learned was that if a little voice tells me to do something, I'm going to pay better attention. I sure wish I had done it that time."

Joyce G., 39, Illinois, Vision Therapy
A family trip is spoiled by an unreliable car.

"WE HAD A WONDERFUL FAMILY VACATION scheduled where we would be going to Cedar Point amusement park in Sandusky, Ohio. As we prepared to leave, I received a very bad feeling about the car we were packing, and seemed to be told that we needed to take the other one because this one wouldn't make the trip. I said to my husband, "Let's take the other car." He would not hear of this and continued packing the original car, but he was sorry later.

We did, in fact, have car trouble just as my little voice had said, when our car refused to slip into gear. It even cost us extra money because we had to stay over in a motel another night while the car was in the shop. I guess maybe my husband will listen better the next time I say that a little voice spoke to me."

"I even had other times where I felt I was receiving special help. When I was driving on a dangerously icy road once, my car went right through a stop sign and I couldn't control it. I prayed, "Oh God, please help me" as I struggled with the steering wheel, and tried to get control.

I know I wasn't steering the car, but it drove smoothly off the road, onto the shoulder, and came to a gentle stop on a grass lawn. I know it wasn't me who performed this feat because I think there was another set of hands on my steering wheel."

Dana D., 21, Minnesota, Secretary
A change in plans prevents a young woman from seeing her fiance.

"IN 1990, I WAS BLISSFULLY ENGAGED to someone, and it was a very happy time for us as we shopped for rings and signed an agreement on a new house. We made plans to meet one weekend since we lived in different cities, and I remember that it was so weird that my fiance Dusty called me an unusual number of times prior to the day we had planned to get together. He didn't typically call that many times.

Because he was coming, I had canceled birthday plans with a very good friend who wasn't terribly happy that I did that. Dusty called me and said that I shouldn't do that to my friend, and since he was going to go home and lie down before driving in, I should go ahead with the birthday plans. I did go, and we had an O.K. time, but he was on my mind too much for me to really enjoy it.

My girlfriend tells me that all of a sudden, around midnight, I turned white as a sheet, started to shake violently, and just didn't want to do anything but get home to see Dusty.

To my surprise, he wasn't in yet, so I left a note for him and went to bed. I feel that I must not have been asleep very long when suddenly Dusty was sitting at the end of my bed, and I thought he had arrived late. He was saying to me,

"I'm so sorry, I never meant for this to happen." I sat up to give him a hug, thinking he was apologizing for being late, when I realized with a shock that I was alone, and what I had seen was simply a mirage or a dream. Or was it?

All I really know is that Dusty's father called me around 2 a.m. and said that Dusty had been killed in a car accident approximately 11:30 on his way to see me. Had he really visited me one last time or had I simply imagined his presence? It took me a long time to stop feeling guilty, thinking that somehow I could have changed what had happened if he had come sooner or if I had not gone out with my friend.

I know now that you cannot change these kinds of things, you just learn to accept them.

LESSONS IN SURRENDER

1. Our own thoughts, needs, and desires are sometimes so strong that we are unwilling to listen to the messages of warning and guidance that we receive.

2. It is important to pay attention to what we are being told and let go of our wish to have things go the way we want them to.

3. In surrendering our wish for control, we must believe that our best interests will be served.

PERSONAL JOURNAL

Think about the following, and record any impressions:

1. Did I ever receive a warning or guidance that I ignored? What happened?

2. How could I be more cognizant in the future of listening for the messages that I need to hear?

INDIVIDUAL INSIGHTS OR OBSERVATIONS ABOUT "SURRENDER" IN THE CIRCUMSTANCES OF MY LIFE:

Write in a journal any thoughts that come to mind.

Are There Really
Just "Coincidences"?

A Lesson in Awareness

HILE MANY OF THE EXAMPLES that people related to me could clearly fit into specific categories such as a warning, or a guiding voice, or even that extra burst of strength when a helping hand was needed, others could not be so easily designated. Some stories were just plain baffling with no logical explanation even with the eyes of faith, and others seemed to need a completely new category called miracle. One of the first stories below clearly fits the miracle category, while others will simply cause you to scratch your head in perplexity wondering, was this a coincidence or not?

Janice L., 46, Minnesota
The doctors placed Janice's file in their "miracle drawer" because they have no explanation.

BEFORE I TELL YOU ABOUT JANICE, I must relate the circumstances of our meeting. Janice attended a seminar I presented, and came up to me to give me a telephone number where I could reach her to hear her story. She said, "I don't have time to do this right now, but I must tell you a story about when I was burned from head to toe many years ago." This statement prompted me to look at her closely, surprised, because she was lovely; there were no outward signs of burn trauma such as scarring, puckering, or wrinkling. Her skin was perfect and healthy and her features were attractive. I couldn't wait to talk to her to find out what had happened.

This is Janice's amazing journey...

"In 1966, my family was renting an older home and my younger brother and I lived with our parents. My bedroom was a porch on the front of the house that had been turned into an extra room, and it had both an outside door and the front door into the main part of the house. On November 20, my brother woke up and thought he heard the wind blowing but it was really flames roaring through the house.

When I awakened, I saw nothing but a wall of flames and since I couldn't open the door to the outside, I went back into the main part of the burning house. In the living room everything was ablaze: the walls, drapes, furniture, and carpeting. I didn't know this then, but because the carpet was burning, every step I took seared the flesh right off my feet and I was so frightened I didn't even feel it at the time.

When I got to the kitchen, the smoke was so thick it clogged my nose and mouth and I couldn't breathe. Somehow I was guided to get down on my hands and knees below the level of the smoke (it's amazing how snippets of emergency information that you have heard over the years just automatically kick in when they are needed...) and I made it out the back door.

In the yard, we greeted each other hysterically as we regrouped. My mother had climbed out a window because the flames were so thick outside her door they had turned her back. My little brother (two years younger) had made it out the kitchen door also. I thought that I had been walking calmly and rationally through the house, but my mother said that it was my frantic, ear-splitting screams that had awakened her and caused her to escape out the window.

My mother realized I was naked because the clothing had been melted right off my back, so she grabbed a rug from the back porch and wrapped it around me. We went to the neighbors who called the emergency vehicles which came within three minutes. The firefighters were shocked that anyone had survived given the seriousness of the involvement of the fire when they arrived.

While I had not been aware of much pain up to this point, I suddenly began to hurt worse than I ever had, and before my eyes swelled completely shut, I noticed that the parts of my body that I could see looked and smelled disgusting. Nothing was recognizable and people were turning away from me with horrified looks on their faces.

In the emergency room, the doctors didn't know where to start to treat the burns, and so I was forwarded to the Burn Center at the university where better facilities existed. Basically, I was unrecognizable and staff could only find two undamaged spots (one on my ankle and one under my arm) where an IV could be inserted. They immediately performed a tracheotomy so I could breathe, and by now, my eyes had almost completely swollen shut. I think the weirdest thing of all was to be asked, "Are you Negro or Caucasian?"

Soon I found that the second-and third-degree burns were over 85%-90% of my body, and although no one informed me of this at the time, the doctors did not expect me to live. Maybe that was why they opted for what was at that time a primarily experimental treatment step: covering me in silver nitrate and wrapping me like a mummy.

I was not allowed to have a mirror, and people had to be prepared to see me. They gave me completely open visiting privileges rather than isolating me as they normally do (to prevent infection) because they were convinced that I would die at any moment. My boyfriend—who later became my husband—said if I was put in a room with a couple of other people and he was asked to pick me out, he would have been unable to do so. I couldn't help but notice that some friends and family members gagged when they saw me and had to leave the room.

It was not a surprise to me, therefore, when I happened to see my reflection in a hallway on the way to x-ray, and saw nothing but a black lump with the circles of my eyes staring out.

After a few days, when I was still hanging in there, doctors realized in surprise that I might survive, so they began other kinds of treatments. The second week, they started peeling off blackened, charred pieces to expose new pink skin underneath. This is an incredibly painful process. Doctors seemed elated at what they saw and commented on how well my own skin was growing after such severe trauma. They started bringing in other specialists and experts to observe me too.

I maintained a positive attitude the whole time, even when they delivered the bad news: I should expect to remain in the university burn center for at least 9-12 months, plan on numerous skin grafting plastic surgeries after that, and still have no guarantee that I would ever again resemble the picture I had to have sent in so they would know what I was supposed to look like. This was very disheartening news but I refused to be set back by it, so I continued to keep my attitude positive.

Maybe that attitude was what accomplished the miracle...

Because the more they pealed, the more I healed, and pink fresh skin rapidly replaced the charred hunks. But that wasn't all! Doctors were exclaiming that something was happening that they had never seen before, and special surgical professionals from all over came to observe it. What occurred was that my body completely regrew its skin in a month!

I was home for Christmas, so less than 4 and ½ weeks after my terrible experience, my body had completely healed. I had regained all of my normal features, and had no scarring at all except for a spot on my shoulder where the back porch rug that my mother had wrapped around me had had sand particles in it. And I do have a couple of places that will flush a bright red if I get overheated. Other than that, I had returned to my former self.

The doctors were frankly, dumbfounded. They had me speak to other patients who were not even as badly injured as I had been but who were in much worse shape. They used me as a model of the "best case" scenario for a burn injury. Many of my friends and some of the hospital staff commented that they believed my absolute refusal to become dispirited had helped stimulate the power of the mind to heal the body.

I think that there may even be more to it, and some of the help came from outside me. Maybe the doctors do too since they filed my case history under a file heading called "Miracles", because there is no medical explanation for my recovery and the doctors cannot say how it happened. It had never happened before to any of them, and they could find no previous example of such a recovery in any of their reference books.

I have lived my life ever since this incident in a way that proclaims, "I have a purpose for being on earth." I don't understand *why* I deserved to have something happen to me that hasn't happened for other burn victims, but it must simply be accepted."

Noreen V., 64, Virginia, Library Consultant
Noreen is reunited with a loved one after 37 years...with tragic results.

NOREEN IS A LOVELY WOMAN of Belgian ancestry who has had a very difficult life and through a series of "coincidences" found one fleeting moment of exquisite happiness before suffering the worst heartbreak she could ever imagine. Her story will move you as much as it did me.

In the early 50s, Noreen was attending college in New Mexico when she met a dashing man—a member of the Apache tribe—and fell in love, marrying him in 1952. They soon had several children, but her marriage turned sour when he became violently abusive and severely beat and tormented her, usually after drinking too much. By 1957, she knew this was intolerable and wanted to get out.

During the time when Noreen felt so lonely and unhappy she wanted to die, another member of the tribe had befriended her, counseled her, supported her emotionally and she fell in love with him. She did not receive any of this flattering attention or kindness at home, and when this man advised her to leave a relationship that was killing her very spirit, she informed her husband that she intended to divorce him. Her husband, of course, reacted with rage and retaliation, and threatened to take the children away from her if she tried to leave him. Now even the threat of this crippled her, because her husband declared that as a non-U.S. citizen, she had no legal rights in this country and could not fight him. Noreen was too terrified to dispute this information, and meekly stopped talking of divorce. She had no relatives in this country, no money, and—she thought—no rights.

Her husband, knowing of her friendship with another man, took the family off the reservation, and they remained married for 28 years, finally splitting up in 1980. All this time, Noreen had never forgotten Charlie, the one best friend she had ever had. They had no contact, although she would periodically ask one of her six kids if they had seen him and if he was alright. Since the town was so small, everyone knew one another, and so she could obtain snippets of information without arousing too much curiosity. He had prospered over the years, been involved in politics, even held the position of tribal Chairman for over twelve years, and had married three times, but apparently never happily. Noreen will tell you about recent events:

"In 1993, I was working on an assignment in London, and in August I began having dreams several nights in a row about Charlie. They were very intense and full of the most ardent yearning to see him again. This feeling almost became more than I could bear, and when I couldn't stand it any longer, I wrote to him. He didn't even seem shocked about hearing from me after more than 35 years but was happy about it, and I found that I wasn't disrupting his life at all, since he had been divorced for nearly 15 years, just about exactly the same amount of time that I had been...

When I returned to the United States in October, I called him and he invited me out to New Mexico for a visit, which I did on October 20. I knew him right away in the airport, even as I saw the years had not been very kind to him. As we got to know one another again over the next few days, the intervening time melted away, and it was almost as if we were young again, even though he was now 72, and I was 64. We walked arm-in- arm around Santa Fe and Durango like 16 year-olds, drove through the glorious vastness of the 350,000 square-mile reservation that I remembered so well, and looked at the sky and dreamed. He loved to drive out and look for eagles and other wildlife.

After I left, we talked every day on the phone and wrote lengthy letters during November and December 1993 and planned for my next visit in January. I stayed for a week towards the end of January and Charlie asked me on one of our rides through the reservation to marry him in the spring, which I agreed to do.

When I returned home, Charlie called me and told me that I had left my coat in the front closet and he would mail it to me the next day. That next day, I called him at 6 p.m. as was our habit, and there was no answer, although I tried several more times before I went to bed. It was a very restless night for me, and I had an extremely disturbing dream: I was approaching Charlie's house and walked inside. Someone was there, but when he turned, this was a person I did not recognize, and he said to me, "Charlie isn't here." "Where did he go?" I asked. "He didn't go anywhere. They came and took him away and you'll never see him again." I woke up screaming, and I knew something was very, very wrong.

When I still couldn't get an answer at Charlie's house the next day, I finally called my daughter Theresa and told her to go over there and to go inside the house. I told her where to find a key, and said if Charlie was there, to simply say that I was worried about him and had told her to go inside to check on him.

My heart nearly stopped when my daughter called with the news: the lights and television were on at the house, but Charlie was dead in his bedroom sprawled half in and half out of his bed. Since he was such a creature of habit, I knew that he had probably died when I called the previous evening. His son had seen him at 4:00 as he returned from mailing my coat, and he always watched television from 5:00 to 6:00, and then turned it off to wait for my call. He must have dozed off during that time and awakened when the phone rang, tried to get up, and had the heart attack right then. I was inconsolable! How could I lose this great love when I had just found it again? We had had only three months!

I did go out to New Mexico for the funeral, but it was very hard. He had given me some of his favorite pictures so I have something to remember him by, but all of his other possessions were buried with him according to Indian custom. Since January 1993, every day has been hard for me.

I want to talk about several very odd incidents since his death, however. Not too long after the funeral, I was playing a tape of Charlie's favorite music, the soundtrack from the movie Last of the Mohicans, and I just fell upon my bed sobbing hysterically. Why, why, why? Abruptly, the tape stopped, and I halted my crying almost as if someone had slapped me. It brought me sharply back to reality. I went to check the tape, and it was in the middle of one of the sides. I fastforwarded to the end, turned it over, and it played normally, and the tape has never since stopped. It was almost like he was scolding me and telling me to stop crying for him.

Recently, I was on assignment in Russia, and had a strange experience in my hotel room. One night, there was a sharp knock on my bedside table, and when I reached over and touched it, it vibrated beneath my hand. There was also a very loud knock on the floor about the same time. One other time, also when I was in Russia, I was lying on my right side, and I could distinctly feel my heart beating. At the same time, I could clearly HEAR underneath my pillow, a heartbeat of a different rhythm. This was very definitely under my head.

Since I have returned to the States, other things have happened. Just a few days ago, I know I felt someone tucking me in and pulling the blanket around me after I had thrown the covers off. I actually felt movements by my legs, back, and shoulders tucking the blanket. I often feel a cool breeze against my forehead when I am meditating or thinking about Charlie.

So, in many ways, I still feel him around me. It was such an unusual thing, so coincidental, that he should come into my life after that long, and it is devastating to lose him this quickly. Every day is a challenge, but all I can do is go on the best I can."

Lynne W., 42, Arizona, Registered Nurse

Lynne "coincidentally" stops at a church and takes a trip down memory lane.

LYNNE RECENTLY EXPERIENCED the most amazing series of coincidences, ones that truly stretch our belief that in any way these could be accidental in their occurrence. She has a 14 year-old daughter who became severely emotionally troubled, and began exhibiting behavioral problems at home and at school. This involved experimentation with drugs and failures in school subjects as well as "acting out" anger and disobedience. Lynne has a relative who is a senior executive in a well-known rehabilitation program for troubled youth, and when Lynne asked for a slot, she was told to get a plane ticket for her daughter and herself and be ready to go as soon as clearance was received.

The particular program that she hoped to enroll her daughter in was on a ship in the Gulf and she needed to board the boat at St. Petersburg, Florida. When she learned that a berth had been obtained, she and her daughter abruptly got on a plane and headed to Florida. She had been given a telephone number to call when she arrived to find out the dock that she needed to go to, but instead she just headed toward the wharf and decided to make the call from there. The first odd coincidence of this trip occurred when she telephoned the contact number and was asked "Where are you?" When she named her location on the quay, she was told, "Turn around to your right, you're already there in the correct place; you should see the boat coming in just about an hour from now exactly where you're waiting." It seemed rather unusual to drive to a huge, unfamiliar port and find precisely the right dock among many ship moorings unless she was somehow led there.

The real coincidences occurred after she left her daughter. It was "emotionally devastating" as Lynne describes it, to put her daughter on that ship, but in her heart she was convinced that it was the right thing to do, and there was simply no other choice. As she drove back into town, she began feeling very sentimental about the city since this was the town she had been born in and lived in when she was young but had not visited in over 30 years. There was no way that she was going to get right back on a plane and go home without seeing some of the places she had memories of. It was Good Friday so she would not be able to stay long, since she needed to get back to her family for Easter.

"I drove by St. Anthony's hospital, where I was born, and then wanted to find the Lutheran church that my minister father had built back in the '50s. When I got there, the church area was deserted, but I walked around for a minute and encountered a woman who was just leaving. She wore a collar, and when I introduced myself, discovered that she was the current pastor. I explained that my father had built the church and I had lived there as a young girl.

The pastor said, "Oh, you're the perfect person to talk to then. We were cleaning a cupboard at the church office today, and we found a large box of old pictures. No one on the staff had any idea who any of these people are, and you may recognize some of them. We were going to throw them away." We went inside, and what a trip down memory lane… This was a box of old black and white pictures of my family. There was the house I was born in, pictures of my brother and younger sister, my mom and dad, my aunt. I was so thrilled to see them, it was almost more than I could bear with the emotional state I was in caused by my current family crisis.

This wonderful woman could see that I was very upset and spent some time counseling with me as I explained what had been going on in my life. It turned out that before the ministry, she had been a nurse for more than 20 years just like me. We talked and prayed together and she spoke about the wonderful healing ministry she is doing now, and I felt better for having encountered her. My parents were astounded when I returned from my trip with a pictorial history of our family.

I felt that it was the weirdest set of coincidences to show up in St. Petersburg after 30 years, on the very day they clean a cupboard at the church. It was significant that I could so easily have missed the pastor since she was just leaving, if I had arrived even a minute after I did. And yet, the encounter I had with her was so comforting for me given the state I was in. So, was it really just coincidences?"

Mary B., 34, Minnesota, Insurance Office Manager

A music box plays for the first time in over 20 years… is it a message from Sue?

"ABOUT A MONTH AFTER I WAS MARRIED, a very dear friend named Sue died of a stroke in July 1992 at just 32 years of age. This was a terrible shock because it was so unexpected—people that age aren't supposed to have a stroke, and they aren't supposed to die.

Sue and I and another friend named Kay had been a kind of "Three Musketeers" gang, and Kay had also experienced a tragedy at about that same time—her father had died a short time prior to Sue. Kay and I were together on the Saturday after Sue's death when a very strange thing happened.

Kay was sitting in the bedroom going through pictures looking for some to use in a collage for the service, and I was in the bathroom curling my hair. Suddenly, a music box on the dresser began to slowly play, building up speed, going faster and faster, until it played through the entire version of "Somewhere my Love." After it finished one complete rendition, it stopped and even though we rewound it, it refused to play again. What was so extraordinary about this is that the music box had not played in over 20 years, despite being jostled about in numerous house moves. It had belonged to my mother who had died in 1971, and had simply never played after her death, but I had always kept it near me for sentimental reasons.

Sue knew how much I loved that music box. Maybe this was just some kind of wild coincidence, and would never happen again in a million years, or maybe it was a sign that Sue was still nearby even though we couldn't touch, see, or speak to her. Somewhere in a very deep part of me, I want to believe that she tried to comfort us, knew of our sorrow and pain, and had sent a sign to help us be strong. It makes it a little easier to bear the sadness that way."

Sue B., 46, Iowa, Dentistry
A young Navy wife senses her husband…is this the moment he was lost at sea?

"TWENTY-FIVE YEARS AGO, I was within days of delivering my baby when a strange thing happened. I woke up on a Tuesday night and had the strongest feeling that my husband was in the room with me. Now, this was physically impossible because he was stationed on the submarine Scorpion which had been at sea for some time. Of course, I missed him terribly, but knew that he was due back in just less than a week, and thought maybe I was feeling close to him because he would be home soon.

Our baby was born on Saturday, and my husband was due back in port the following Monday, so he would have a new child to greet him. Except...he didn't return...

My husband's ship was lost at sea, but they didn't really know for about six months approximately where or when the loss occurred because the sub was on radio silence during the return trip. In some papers that I obtained access to over the years, I have since learned that the Navy believes the sub went down just about the time that I had felt that odd presence of my husband in the house. I think he had come back spiritually to be with us for a little while right when he died."

Yvonne P., 33, Arizona, State Government

An ultrasound machine brought to a room "for no reason" is the clue to the problem with Yvonne's baby.

"WHILE I THINK THERE MAY BE indeed be such a thing as a coincidence in our lives, I know that what happened to me when my baby was born was no accident. Three years ago, when my son was ready to come into this world, I was at a military hospital, already two weeks overdue. My doctor had decided that it was time to induce labor, but when he was ready to start, he couldn't find the person who had the key to the cabinet where the drugs were stored.

While I was lying in the bed waiting, some staff person wheeled in an ultrasound machine on a cart and parked it in the corner. It didn't appear to have anything to do with me, it seemed as if she simply needed a place to get the machine out of the way. No one else was in the room, so there wouldn't be any particular reason to bring it in.

My doctor came in and was sitting and waiting, making small talk with me. He seemed impatient and a little frustrated at the delay because he wanted to get the drug started. As we began to have more pauses than conversation, he said offhandedly and almost as an afterthought, "Why don't we take a minute to do an ultrasound since that machine happens to be here?"

Well, what a shock as the picture came into view! The baby was breeched with the feet way back over the head! The decision was made right at that moment to do a caesarean section. The doctor seemed stunned since there had been no indication before that that the baby had rotated into such a position.

It distressed me that we had been ready to induce active labor which would have created some tremendous difficulties with the delivery and may even have harmed the baby. I don't think it was an accident that the ultrasound machine appeared in the room although the doctor had not requested it. Someone knew that my baby was in trouble and that we needed to find out about it. All of the strange "coincidences" that came together at the same time—the machine being parked there, the delay in starting, the impatient doctor—could so easily not have occurred."

LESSONS IN AWARENESS

1. Because events that appear as coincidences are in some cases potentially able to be explained away, we may not always recognize them as the heaven-sent circumstances they really are.

2. We must increase our awareness of small signs or situations where things are occurring in our favor.

3. If we believe that something unusual or beneficial has happened, then we must continue to believe it even if others say that it is "only luck" or a "happy coincidence." The word "co-incidence" itself could be interpreted as a sense of partnership or someone "with" us in an incident, a sharing of a set of circumstances.

4. If we expect that miracles will occur, it is far more likely that they will.

PERSONAL JOURNAL

Think about the following, and record any impressions:

1. Have extremely fortunate or seemingly "lucky" things happened to me? How did I explain the circumstances? Did others agree or disagree?

2. How can I be more aware to look for the situations where something helpful or beneficial will occur?

INDIVIDUAL INSIGHTS OR OBSERVATIONS ABOUT "AWARENESS" IN THE CIRCUMSTANCES OF MY LIFE:

Write in a journal any thoughts that come to mind.

~ *Conclusion* ~

WHILE THE STORIES IN THIS VOLUME have been categorized for ease of reading, I believe that human experiences of angelic intervention cannot really be defined, explained, examined under a microscope, or put into classifications because each one is so unique and personal. The ultimate question is "What does it do for the growth, development, nourishment, or protection of the person"? How is one individual's life changed in a way in which it makes a difference to the planet? If someone feels a strengthening of faith, blossoming of hope and deepening of courage by taking the hand of an angel, then all of the human species is just a little stronger.

In the haste today to scientifically explain all events, we don't leave room for the unexplainable, the "wondrous" occurrence that can only be understood with an eye of faith. The more we are willing to accept these sometimes "miraculous" phenomena and to talk about them openly, the more frequent they are becoming. The angels are definitely moving upon the earth in a more visible fashion in this age, and our reaction to that must be one of gratitude.

As a reader of this book, you have had an opportunity to be inspired by the experiences of real people, and to reflect on how some of these same things may have occurred in your own life. At the very least, you may be more aware in the future of how to take advantage of the power available to you when you take the hand of an angel.

∽ *Index* ∽

To help you find your story...